PREPARE YOUR OWN
LAST WILL AND TESTAMENT-
WITHOUT A LAWYER

By

Daniel Sitarz

Attorney-at-Law

NOVA PUBLISHING COMPANY

CARBONDALE, ILLINOIS

Manufactured in the United States.

Library of Congress Catalog Card Number 86-63265

ISBN 00-935755-01-2

Library of Congress Cataloging-in-Publication Data

    Prepare Your Own Last Will and Testament—Without a Lawyer
    (Legal Self-Help Series) Includes Index
    1. Wills--United States--Popular Works. 2. Wills--United States--Forms. I. Title. II. Series.
    KF755.Z9S49 1988 346.7305'4 86-63265 347.30654 ISBN 0-935755-01-2 (pbk)

This publication is designed to provide accurate and authoritative information in regard to the subject matter covered. It is sold with the understanding that the publisher and author are not engaged in rendering legal, accounting or other professional services. If legal advice or other expert assistance is required, the services of a competent professional person should be sought.

> - From a Declaration of Principles jointly adopted by a Committee of the American Bar Association and a Committee of Publishers.

DISCLAIMER

Because of possible unanticipated changes in governing statutes and case law relating to the application of any information contained in this book, the author, publisher, and any and all persons or entities involved in any way in the preparation, publication, sale or distribution of this book disclaim all responsibility for the legal effects or consequences of any document prepared or action taken in reliance upon any information contained in this book. No representations, either express or implied, are made or given regarding the legal consequences of the use of any information contained in this book. Purchasers and persons intending to use this book for the preparation of any legal documents are advised to check specifically on the current applicable laws and statutes in any jurisdiction in which they intend the document to be effective.

NOVA PUBLISHING COMPANY

CARBONDALE, ILLINOIS

• TABLE OF CONTENTS •

INTRODUCTION

This book is intended to serve as a guide and explanation to its readers of the processes and legal techniques required in preparing a valid Last Will and Testament without the aid of an attorney. It is part of NOVA Publishing Company's continuing series on Legal Self-Help. These self-help legal guides are prepared by licensed Attorneys who feel that public access to the American legal system is long overdue.

Many areas of law are easily understood and applied by the average person in today's world. Preparing your own valid Will is one of these areas. Understandably, there is strong resistance by many lawyers against making this information available to the public. Many lawyer's jobs depend upon doing things that their clients could do just as well, if the clients had access to the proper information. There has been, in the past, a concerted effort on the part of the organized Bar and other lawyer organizations to prevent "self-help" legal information, such as is contained in this book, from reaching the general public. This effort has gone hand-in-hand with an effort to leave the Law cloaked in antiquated and unnecessary legal language which, of course, one must pay a lawyer to translate.

Law in American society today is far more pervasive than ever before. There are legal consequences to virtually every public and most private actions in today's society. Leaving knowledge of the Law within the hands of only the lawyers in such a society is not only foolish but dangerous as well. This book and others in NOVA's Legal Self-Help Series are intended to provide the necessary information to those members of the public who wish to use and understand the Law for themselves.

This book is designed to assist its readers in understanding the general aspects of the law as it relates to Wills and after-death distribution of property and to assist its readers in the preparation of their own Wills. However, the range of personal finances, property, and desires is infinite and one book can not hope to cover all potential situations or contingencies. In situations involving complex personal or business property holdings, situations involving complicated or substantial financial investments, or in situations involving unusual or highly-complex post-death distribution plans, readers are advised to seek additional competent legal advice. In addition, estate and inheritance tax laws and regulations are among the most complex and rapidly-changing laws in existence. Consequently, although a general overview of these laws is provided and the vast majority of people are exempt from Federal Estate Taxes, readers with very large estates or complex financial resources are encouraged to seek the assistance of a tax professional if they wish to limit or lessen the tax consequences of the transfer of any property using a Will.

To try and make your task as easy as possible, technical legal jargon has been eliminated whenever possible and plain English used instead. When it is necessary to use a legal term which may be unfamiliar to most people, it will be shown in *italics* and defined when first used. There is a glossary of most legal terms used in Wills at the end of this book for your reference in deciphering your current Will if it was prepared by an Attorney using outdated technical legal language. Lawyers love to caution people that such antiquated language is most important and that, of course, only they, the lawyers, can properly prepare and interpret legal documents using such language. Naturally, plain and easily-understood English is not only perfectly proper for use in all legal documents, but in most cases, leads to far less confusion on the part of later readers. The only drawback to using plain English for preparing legal documents is that it may place a few more lawyers on the unemployment lines.

Chapter 1 of this guide will attempt to explain the usefulness and in many cases the necessity of a valid Will for insuring that your property and money are passed on to the loved ones that you desire. It will also explain the legal effects of having a Will and the potential consequences of not having a Will.

Chapter 2 provides guidelines for planning for the effective and desired disposition of your property and money after your death. This Chapter also includes an overview of information relating to the *probate* (court administration) of your Estate, and the inheritance and estate tax consequences of the transfer of property at death. Your *estate* consists of all of the assets that you own at the time of your death. In addition, included are an explanation of the qualifications necessary for having a Will and who may be a *beneficiary* (one who benefits or receives a gift through a Will), and a discussion of what property may be disposed of using a Will.

A step-by-step outline of the procedures to follow to prepare your own Will using this book is provided in Chapter 3.

A detailed Personal Questionnaire is provided in Chapter 4 which will allow you to assemble the necessary personal and financial information which you will need in preparing your Will.

Sample fill-in-the-blank Will clauses are contained in Chapter 5 for use in preparing your own personally-tailored Will. An explanation of each clause and instructions on how to properly fill them in are also provided. The included clauses should be sufficient for most people and most circumstances.

An actual sample Will is shown and its various provisions are explained in Chapter 6.

The mechanics of actually preparing your Will are set forth in Chapter 7.

The legal formalities and requirements for signing your Will are contained in Chapter 8. These requirements, although not at all difficult, must be followed precisely to insure that your Will is acceptable as a valid legal document. Methods and instructions for safeguarding your Will are also contained in this chapter.

Chapter 9 contains information regarding when it may be prudent and how to accomplish any changes or alterations to your Will at a later date.

Chapter 10 provides an explanation and form for your preparation of a "Living" Will--a document directing that, if you are diagnosed as terminally ill, no extraordinary life support measures be instituted to artificially prolong your life.

The Appendix contains a detailed listing of the individual state legal requirements relating to Wills for each of the 50 states and the District of Columbia.

Finally, a Glossary of legal terms most often encountered in Wills is included.

As with many routine legal tasks, preparation of a Will is not as difficult as most people fear. With the proper information before them, most people will be able to prepare a legally valid Will which addresses their individual needs in a matter of a few hours. Read through this manual carefully, follow the step-by-step instructions and be assured that your wishes will be safely contained in your own Last Will and Testament.

CHAPTER 1

Why Do You Need a Will?

For most of us, it is very difficult to come to terms with our own mortality. To actually contemplate one's own death is painful. Consequently, such thoughts are generally avoided. However, if you wish to insure that your desires regarding the disposition of your property and possessions after your death are fulfilled, you must confront your mortality and plan accordingly.

Most people's lives are centered on living, and, in one way or another, on a close and intimate group of loved ones. These may be relatives, friends, church members, or business associates. They are looked to for love, support, and assistance in times of trouble and are often asked to share in times of joy. They are often cared about in ways that are difficult to express. But during your life, you at least have the opportunity to show your love and concern in many forms.

It is the purpose of this book to assist you in the difficult task of showing these loved ones your continuing concern for their well-being after you are gone. "You can't take it with you" is a well-worn phrase, but it does strike to the core of the problem of the necessity of providing for your property and money to be distributed in some fashion on your death. Your entire life has been spent accumulating possessions and wealth for your own comfort and the comfort of your loved ones. Through the proper use of a Will, you have a once-in-a-lifetime opportunity to personally decide what will happen to your accumulated wealth and possessions when you are gone. It is your entirely personal decision. Indeed, it is your legal privilege to make this decision. No one but you has the power to decide, prior to your death, how and to whom your property should be distributed on your demise. But to do so, you must take the initiative and overcome the understandable difficulty of these decisions. If you do not take the initiative and prepare your own Will, on your death an impersonal court will decide who will receive your wealth.

To actually sit down and decide how your property and possessions should be divided amongst your loved ones in the event of your own death is not an easy task. However, it is you alone who knows your wishes. The property and possessions that you own may be land, your home, your personal household furnishings, keepsakes, heirlooms, money, stocks, bonds, or any other type of property. It may be worth thousands of dollars or it may be worth far less. If you are like most people, you want to insure that it is passed on to the persons whom you choose. But again, if you are like most people, you have put off making a Will. Nearly 75% of Americans are without a valid Will.

A Will or *Last Will and Testament*, as such document is formally titled, is a legal document that, when accepted by the probate court, is proof of an intent to transfer property to the persons or organizations named in the Will upon the death of the maker of the Will. The maker of the Will is known as the *Testator*. A Will is effective for the transfer of property that is owned by the Testator on the date of his death. A Will can be changed, modified, or revoked at any time by the Testator prior to death.

It is equally important to understand that for a Will to be valid, it must generally be prepared, witnessed and signed according to certain technical legal procedures. Although a Will is perfectly valid if it is written in plain English and does not use technical legal language, it MUST be prepared, witnessed, and signed in the manner outlined in this book. This can not be overemphasized. You can not take any shortcuts when following the instructions as they relate to the procedures necessary for completing and signing your Will. These procedures are not at all difficult and consist generally of carefully typing your Will in the manner outlined later, signing it in the manner specified, and having three witnesses and a notary public also sign the document. (Although not a legal requirement, the notarization of your Will will aid in its proof later). [NOTE: Louisiana residents must follow the procedures noted at the end of Chapter 7].

In the past, it was in many cases possible to simply write down your wishes, sign the paper, and be confident that your wishes would be followed upon your death. Unfortunately, this is, in most cases, no longer possible. *Holographic* (or handwritten and unwitnessed) Wills are no longer accepted as valid in most jurisdictions. *Nuncupative* (or oral) Wills are also not admissible in most probate courts to prove a person's intent to dispose of property on death. For this reason, a valid, typewritten Will which is prepared, signed, and witnessed according to formal legal requirements is now essentially the only secure method to assure the desired disposition of your property, possessions, and money after your death and to assure that your loved ones are taken care of according to your final wishes.

In some cases (for example, those involving extremely complicated business or personal financial holdings or the desire to create a complex trust arrangement) it is clearly advisable to consult an attorney for the preparation of your Will. However, in most circumstances and for most people, the terms of a Will which will provide for the necessary protection are relatively routine and may safely be prepared without the added expense of consulting a lawyer.

REASONS FOR HAVING A WILL.

There are many reasons why it is desirable to have a Will. Perhaps most important is to insure that it is YOU who decides how your estate is distributed on your death and to be assured that those loved ones whom you wish to share in your bounty actually receive your gifts.

TO AVOID HAVING THE STATE DECIDE
WHO WILL RECEIVE YOUR PROPERTY.

What happens to your property and possessions if you do not have a valid and legal Will or if the Will that you have is found by the probate court to be invalid because it was not signed or witnessed properly? Law books are filled with many unfortunate cases in which because of the lack of a formal and valid Will, the true desires and wishes of a person as to who should inherit their property have been frustrated. If there is no valid Will to use for direction, a probate judge must give a person's property to either the

11

spouse, children, or the closest blood relatives of the deceased person. This result is required even in situations when it is perfectly clear that the deceased person did not, under any circumstances, want those relatives to inherit the property. Although the probate judge is required to interpret a Will to best satisfy what appears to be the written intentions of the person who signed it, the judge must first have before him a valid Will.

To be valid, the document must, generally, have been signed and witnessed in a formal manner and prepared in such a way as to satisfy certain legal requirements. These requirements are strictly enforced to ensure that the document presented to a probate court is, indeed, the real and valid Will of the deceased person whose property is to be divided.

Without such a valid Will before him or her, a judge must rely on a legislative scheme which has been devised to make for an orderly distribution of property in all cases where there is no valid Will. This scheme is present as law, in one form or another, in all 50 states and is generally referred to as *intestate distribution*.

The terms of this state intestate distribution plan are typically similar in most states. In general, a person's spouse is first in line to receive the property when there is no Will at death. Most states provide that the spouse and/or children will either share the entire estate or the surviving spouse will take it all in the hopes that the spouse will share it with the children. Generally, the spouse will receive one-half and the children will receive one-half. In many states, if a person dies without a valid Will and is survived by a spouse and not by any children, the spouse will inherit the entire estate and the surviving parents, brother, sisters and any other blood relatives to the deceased will be entitled to nothing.

If there is no surviving spouse or children, the blood relatives of the deceased will receive the estate. If there is someone or several persons within the next closest relationship level (for example, grand-parents or brothers or sisters) who is alive on the death of the person, then these relatives will receive all of the person's property or share it equally with all others alive that are in a similar relationship level. Once a level of blood relationship is found in which there is at least one living person, all persons who are more distantly related inherit nothing.

In addition, these legislative distribution plans are set up on the assumption that family members are the only parties that a deceased person would wish to have inherit his or her property. Thus, without a Will, it is impossible to leave any gifts to close friends, in-laws, blood relatives more distant then any alive, charities, or organizations of any type. If there is no Will and if there are no blood relatives alive, the state confiscates all of a person's property under a legal doctrine entitled *escheat*.

As an example of a typical legislative intestate distribution scheme, the following is a general outline of the various levels of blood relationships that are set up in most states:

1. Spouse.

2. Children and parents.

3. Brothers, sisters and grandparents.

4. Aunts, uncles, nephews, nieces, and great-grandparents.

5. Great uncles, great aunts, first cousins, and great-great grandparents.

Many disastrous consequences can result from having your property distributed according to a standardized state plan. Take, for example, a situation in which a person and his or her spouse die from injuries sustained in a single accident, but one spouse survives a few hours longer. If there is no Will, the result in this scenario is that the property of the first one to die passes to the spouse who survives. A few hours later, on the death of the surviving spouse, the property automatically passes only to the relatives of the spouse who survived the longest. The relatives of the first to die can inherit nothing at all. This, obviously would not normally be the desired consequence. Under the typical state scheme, luck and chance play a large role in deciding who is to inherit property.

Each state has a complicated and often different method for deciding which particular blood relatives will take property when there is no will. However, the results are often far from the desires of how the person actually wished to have the property distributed. Obviously, under this type of state distribution of your property, the individual circumstances of your family are not taken into consideration at all nor are any intentions that you may have had, regardless of how strongly you may have expressed them during your lifetime. The only way to avoid having the state decide who is to receive your property is to have prepared a legally valid Will. If you die without a valid Will, the state essentially writes one for you on its terms.

TO APPOINT YOUR OWN CHOICE AS TO WHO SHOULD ADMINISTER THE DIVISION OF YOUR PROPERTY.

Another very important reason for having a Will is the ability to appoint an executor of your own choice. An *Executor* is your personal representative for seeing that your wishes, as contained in your Will, are carried out after your death and that your taxes and debts are paid. An executor also collects and inventories all of your property and is in charge of seeing that it is distributed according to your wishes as expressed in your Will. Typically, a spouse or a brother or sister, or other close family member or trusted friend is chosen to act as executor. However, it may be any responsible adult that you would feel confident having this duty. It may even be a local bank or trust company. In that case, of course, there will be an often substantial fee charged to your estate for the completion of these generally routine duties by the corporate executor. If you choose an individual, he or she should be a resident of your home state. The Will clauses in Chapter 5 will enable you to appoint your executor and an alternate executor so that, in the event your first choice can not perform, it is still your personal choice as to who will administer your Will.

If you do not have a Will or if you do not choose an executor in your Will, the probate court judge will appoint someone to administer the distribution of your property.

TO APPOINT A GUARDIAN FOR YOUR MINOR CHILDREN.

For those with minor children, the appointment of a guardian for the children through a Will is another very important item which may be accomplished. A *guardian "of the person"*, as this type of guardian is usually referred to, is responsible for the actual care, custody, and upbringing of a child. If your spouse is alive, he or she would generally be appointed as guardian in any event, with or without a Will. However, there is the possibility that you both will be killed in a single accident or catastrophe.

Also, if you are a single parent, you will need to designate a choice for guardian. Without a Will for direction, a probate judge has little guidance in choosing the person whom you feel would be the best alternative for caring for your children. With a Will, however, you can appoint a guardian for just such an eventuality.

TO APPOINT A GUARDIAN OR TRUSTEE TO ADMINISTER PROPERTY FOR A MINOR CHILD

You can also have such a guardian administer the property or money which you leave to your children (a *guardian "of the property"*), or you may set up a trust and appoint a trustee to administer your children's inheritance until a time when you feel that they will be able to handle their own affairs. A *trust* consists of assets which are managed and distributed by a *trustee* to benefit one or more beneficiaries. Instructions to provide for these alternatives are simply stated in a Will, but are impossible to accomplish without one. If such is not provided for in a Will, and a minor child is left money or property by way of the state intestate succession laws, the courts will generally decide who should administer the property. Such court supervised guardianship of the property or money will automatically end at the child's reaching the legal age of majority in the state (usually 18 years of age). At this age, without a Will to direct otherwise, the child will receive full control over the property and/or money. This may not be the most prudent result, in as much as many 18 year-olds are not capable of managing property or large sums of money. With a Will, it is easy to arrange for the property or money to be held in trust and used to benefit the child until a later age, perhaps 21, 25, or even 30 years of age.

TO DISINHERIT A CHILD OR OTHER RELATIVE.

Disinheritance of a child or other relative whom you feel is not deserving of your property, or has no need of your property, is also something that can be accomplished only through the use of a Will. Although the total disinheritance of a spouse is not possible under the laws of any state, any other relative may, generally, be cut off without a penny from your estate through the use of a Will. [NOTE: In Louisiana, children also may not be totally disinherited.]

TO ACCOMPLISH OTHER RESULTS.

Many other things may be accomplished only through the use of a Will. You can forgive a debt which is owed to you in your Will. You can revoke any other previous Wills. You can provide instructions for organ donations, the disposition of your body, and burial, although it is generally wise to also leave these instructions with your executor on a separate sheet. Additionally, the proper use of a Will normally lessens the expenses of probate, since the disposition of all of your property has been planned in advance, by you.

Although it can be short and simple, a Will is an important document which can accomplish many tasks. The proper use of a Will can eliminate much confusion for those left behind. As it provides a clear and legal record of your wishes, it can avoid feuding and squabbles among your family members. Perhaps most importantly, it can make your last wishes come true.

CHAPTER 2

Planning Your Will

Before actually planning your Will, an overview of how the legal system operates after a person's death may be useful to keep in mind. The system of court administration of the estates of deceased parties is generally entitled *Probate*. How to avoid the probate court was the subject of one of the first self-help law books to challenge the legal establishment's monopoly on law. Probate, however, despite what many lawyers would have you believe, is not all that mysterious a matter.

OVERVIEW OF A TYPICAL PROBATE PROCEEDING.

Upon a person's death in most states, there is a general sequence of events which takes place. First, the Executor appointed in the Will (who, hopefully, has been notified of his duties in advance) locates the Will and files it with the proper authority. If necessary, the Executor arranges for the funeral and burial. If it is a complicated or very large estate, it may be prudent to hire a lawyer to handle the probate proceeding. Upon presenting the Will to the probate court, the Will is *proved*, which means that it is determined whether or not the document presented is actually the deceased's Will. This may be done in most states with a "Self-Proving Affidavit" which is prepared and notarized at the time your Will is signed (See Chapter 5).

Upon proof that it is a valid Will, the Executor is officially given legal authority to gather together all of the estate's property. This authority for the Executor to administer the estate is generally referred to as *letters testamentary*. The probate court also officially appoints the parties who are designated as guardians of any minor children and any trustees.

If no Executor was chosen in the Will, or if the one chosen can not serve, the probate court will appoint one. The order of preference for appointment is commonly as follows: surviving spouse, next of kin, a person having an interest in the estate or claims against the estate.

If the Will is shown to be invalid, or if there is no Will, the same sequence of events generally is followed. However, in this case, the party appointed to administer the estate is usually titled an *Administrator* of the estate rather than an Executor. The court orders granting authority to an Administrator are generally referred to as *letters of administration*.

After the Executor or Administrator is given authority, he or she handles the collection of assets, the management of the estate, and the payment of any debts and taxes until such time as all creditor's claims have been satisfied and other business of the estate completed. An inventory of all of the assets is typically the first official act of an Executor. Creditors, by the way, only have a certain time period in which to make a claim against an estate. The same holds true for any *contests* of the will (challenging the validity of a Will). Contesting a Will is a fairly rare occurrence and is most difficult if the Will was properly prepared and signed by a competent, sane adult.

The Executor will generally also be empowered under state law to provide an allowance for the surviving spouse and children until such time as all affairs of the deceased person are completed and the estate is closed.

Upon completion of all business and payment of all outstanding charges against the estate, an accounting and inventory of the estate's assets are then presented to the probate court by the Executor. At this time, if everything appears to be in order, the Executor is generally empowered to distribute all of the remaining property to the persons or organizations named in the Will and probate is officially closed. The entire probate process generally takes from 4 to 18 months to complete. The distribution of your property and money is usually handled solely by the Executor (possibly with a lawyer's help to be certain that all legal requirements are fulfilled). Normally, this is done without further court approval of the disbursement.

FEDERAL ESTATE TAXES AND STATE INHERITANCE TAXES.

With regard to taxes, recent changes in the Federal Income Tax Code, as it relates to Estate Taxes, have released an estimated 95% of the American public from any Federal Estate Tax liability on their death.

The current IRS rules provide for the equivalent of an exemption from all Estate Tax for the first $600,000.00 of a person's assets. In addition, all of the value of a person's estate that is left to a spouse is exempt from any Federal Estate Tax. Even if your particular assets are over this minimum exemption, there are still methods to lessen or eliminate your tax liability. These methods, however, are beyond the scope of this book. Therefore, if your assets (or your joint assets, if married) total over approximately $600,000.00, it is recommended that you consult a tax professional prior to preparing your Will.

State inheritance taxes are, as a rule, also very minimal or even non-existent until the value of your estate is over $600,000.00. Many state's tax laws are tied directly to the Federal Tax situation and thus allow for the same level of exemption equivalent from state taxes on death if the estate property totals under $600,000.00.

From a planning standpoint, these changes in the Federal Estate Tax have virtually eliminated any consideration of tax consequences from the preparation of a Will for most Americans. Other factors, however, will affect the planning of your Will.

QUALIFICATIONS FOR HAVING A WILL.

Are you legally qualified to have a Will? In general, if you are over 18 years of age and of "sound mind", you will qualify. There are a few states which have different minimum ages, some allowing Wills by children as young as 14, and some requiring the Testator to be 21. For the specific age requirements, check your own state's age requirements in the Appendix.

It is also important to understand that laws of different states may apply to a single Will. The laws of the state in which you have your principal residence will be used to decide the validity of the Will as to any personal property and real estate located in that state. However, if any real estate outside of your home state is mentioned in the Will, then the laws of the state in which that real estate is found will govern the disposition of that particular real estate. Thus, if you own property outside of the state where you live, when you check the Appendix for information concerning specific state laws, be certain to check both your own state's laws and those of the state in which your other property is located.

The requirement to have a "sound mind" refers to the ability to understand the following:

- That you are signing a Will,

- That you know who your beneficiaries are,

- That you understand the nature and extent of your assets.

Having a "sound mind" refers only to the moment when you actually execute the Will. A person who is suffering from a mental illness, or a person who uses drugs or alcohol, or even a person who is senile may legally sign a Will. This is acceptable as long as the Will is signed and understood during a period when the person is lucid and has sufficient mental ability to understand the extent of his or her property, who is to receive that property, and that it is a Will that is being signed.

The fact that a person has a physical incapacity makes no difference in their right to sign a Will. Regardless if a person is blind, deaf, can not speak, is very physically weak, or is illiterate; as long as they understand what it is they are doing and what they are signing, the "sound mind" requirement is met.

Related to the requirement that the Testator have a "sound mind" at the time of signing the Will is the requirement that the Will be signed without any undue influence, fraud, or domination by others. In other words, the Will must be freely signed and reflect the wishes of the person signing it for it to be legally valid.

WHO MAY BE A BENEFICIARY?

Any person or organization who receives property under a Will is termed a *beneficiary* of that Will. Much the same as there are certain requirements that the person signing the Will must meet, there are certain requirements relating to who may receive property under a Will. These generally, however, are in the form of negative requirements. Stated in another way, this means that anyone may receive property under a Will unless they fall into certain narrow categories. These few categories of disqualified beneficiaries are as follows:

- An attorney who drafts the Will is generally assumed to have used undue influence if he or she is made a beneficiary.

- Some states disqualify any witnesses to the execution of the Will. Check the Appendix to see if your state has this restriction. However, to be safe, it is recommended that none of your witnesses be beneficiaries under your Will.

- A person who murders a Testator is universally disqualified from receiving any property under the murdered person's Will.

- An unincorporated association is typically not allowed to receive property under a Will. This particular disqualification stems from the fact that such associations generally have no legal right to hold property.

Besides these few noted exceptions, anyone else may receive property under your Will. This includes the named Executor, any illegitimate children (if named specifically), corporations, creditors, debtors, and any friends, acquaintances, or even strangers.

A few states have restrictions on the right to leave property to charitable organizations and churches. These restrictions are usually in two forms: a time limit prior to death when changes to a Will which leave large amounts of money or property to a charitable organization are disallowed and also a percentage limit on the amount of a person's estate which may be left to a charitable organization (often a limit of 50%). The reasoning behind this rule is to prevent abuse of a dying person's desire to be forgiven. There have, in the past, been unscrupulous individuals or organizations who have obtained last minute changes in a Will in an attempt to have the bulk of a person's estate left to them or their group. If you intend to leave large sums of money or property to a charitable organization or church, please check the Appendix to see if there are any restrictions of this type in force in your state.

Under this same category as to who may be a beneficiary under your Will are several points related to marriage, divorce, and children. First and foremost, you are advised to review your Will periodically and make any necessary changes as your marital or family situation may dictate. If you are divorced, married, remarried, or widowed, adopt or have a child, there may be unforeseen consequences based on the way you have written your Will. Each state has differing laws on the effect of marriage and divorce on a person's Will. In some states, divorce entirely revokes a Will as to the divorced spouse. In others, divorce has no effect and your divorced spouse may inherit your estate if you do not change your Will. Marriage and the birth of children are also treated somewhat differently by each state. You are advised to review the Appendix as it relates to these aspects of your life and prepare your Will accordingly.

Your Will should be prepared with regard to how your life is presently arranged. It should, however, always be reviewed and updated each time there is a substantial change in your life.

WHAT PROPERTY MAY YOU DISPOSE OF WITH YOUR WILL?

In general, you may dispose of any property that you own at the time of your death. This simple fact, however, contains certain factors which require further explanation. There are forms of property which you may "own", but which may not be transferred by way of a Will. In addition, you may own only a percentage or share of certain other property. In such situations, only that share or percentage which you actually own may be left by your Will. Finally, there are types of property ownership which are automatically transferred to another party at your death, regardless of the presence of a Will.

In the first category of property which can not be transferred by Will are properties which have a designated beneficiary outside of the provisions of your Will. These types of properties include:

- life insurance policies;

- retirement plans;

- IRA's and KEOGH's;

- pension plans;

- trust bank accounts;

- payable-on-death accounts;

- U.S. Savings Bonds, with payable-on-death beneficiaries.

In general, if there is already a valid determination of who will receive the property upon your death (as there is, for example, in the choice of a life insurance beneficiary), you may not alter this choice of beneficiary through the use of your Will. If you wish to alter your choice of beneficiary in any of these cases, please directly alter the choice with the holder of the particular property (for instance, the life insurance company).

The next category of property which may have certain restrictions is property in which you may only own a certain share or percentage. Examples of this may be a partnership interest in a company or venture. Using a Will, you may only leave that percentage or fraction of the ownership of the property that is actually yours.

Another example is a spouse's share of marital property in states which follow "Community Property" designation of certain jointly owned property. If you are single, please disregard this section and use the "Common Law Property States" rules below to determine your ownership rights.

Community Property States

Several states, mostly in the Western United States, follow the "community property" type of marital property system. Please refer to the Appendix to see if your state has this type of system. The system itself is derived from ancient Spanish law. It is a relatively simple concept. All property owned by either spouse during a marriage is divided into two types: separate property and community property.

Separate property consists of all property considered owned entirely by one spouse. Separate property, essentially, is all property owned by the spouse prior to the marriage and kept separate during the marriage; and all property received individually by the spouse by gift or inheritance during the marriage. All other property is considered "community property". In other words, all property acquired during the marriage by either spouse, unless by gift or inheritance, is "community property". "Community property" is considered to be owned in equal shares by each spouse, regardless of whose efforts actually went into acquiring the property. (One major exception to this general rule is Social Security benefits, which are considered to be separate property by Federal law).

Thus, if you are a married resident of a "community property" state, the property which you may dispose of by Will consists of all of your "separate" property and one-half of your jointly-owned marital "community property". The other half of the "community property" automatically becomes your spouse's sole property on your death.

Common Law Property States

Residents of all other states are governed by a "common law" property system, which was derived from English law. Under this system, there is no rule which gives fifty percent ownership of the property acquired during marriage to each spouse.

In "common law" states, the property which you may dispose of with your Will consists of all the property held by title in your name and any property which you have earned or purchased with your own money and any property which you may have been given as a gift or inherited, either before or after your marriage.

If your name alone is on a title document in these states (for instance, a deed or automobile title), then you own it solely. If your name and your spouse's name is on the document, you generally own it as "tenant's-in-common", unless it specifically states that your ownership is to be as "joint tenants" or if your state allows for a "tenancy by the entireties" (a form of "joint tenancy"

24

between married persons). There is an important difference between these types of "joint" ownership: namely, survivorship.

With property owned as "tenants-in-common", the percentage or fraction that each "tenant-in-common" owns is property which may be disposed of under a Will. If the property is held as "joint tenants" or as "tenants-by-the entireties", the survivor automatically receives the deceased party's share. Thus, in your Will, you may not dispose of any property held in "joint tenancy" or "tenancy-by-the entirety" since it already has a legal disposition upon your death.

In "common-law" states, you may dispose of any property which has your name on the title in whatever share that the title gives you, unless the title is held specifically as "joint tenants" or "tenants-by-the entireties". You may also dispose of any property which you earned or purchased with your own money, and any property which you have been given as a gift or inherited.. If you are married, however, there is a further restriction on your right to dispose of property by Will.

All "common law" states protect spouses from total disinheritance by providing a statutory scheme under which a spouse may choose to take a minimum share of the deceased partner's estate, regardless of what the Will states. This effectively prevents any spouse from being entirely disinherited through the use of the "common law" rules of property (name on the title = ownership of property).

In most states, the spouse has a right to a one-third share of the deceased spouse's estate, regardless of what the deceased spouse's Will states. However, all states are slightly different in how they apply this type of law and some allow a spouse to take up to one-half of the estate. Please check your particular state's laws in the Appendix. The effect of these statutory provisions is to make it impossible to disinherit a spouse entirely. If you choose to leave nothing to your spouse under your Will or by other means (such as life insurance or joint tenancies), he or she may take it anyway, generally from any property which you tried to leave to others.

Some states also allow a certain "family allowance" or "homestead allowance" to the spouse or children to insure that they are not abruptly cut off from their support by any terms of a Will. These allowances are generally of short duration and for relatively minor amounts of money and differ greatly from state to state.

To review the important points to consider before you begin to prepare your Will:

- You are generally qualified to prepare your own Will if you are over 18 and are of "sound mind". If you have read this far in this book, you may assume that you are of "sound mind". Please, however, check the Appendix for your state's specific age requirements.

- You essentially may leave your property to anyone or any organization, except that you are cautioned against leaving property to anyone who acts as a witness to your Will or to an unincorporated association. You are also advised to consult the Appendix to determine if your state has any restrictions on gifts in a Will to charitable organizations.

- The property which you may dispose of is as follows:

  - In Community Property States: All separate property (property which was brought into a marriage, or obtained by gift or inheritance during the marriage) and one-half of the community property (all other property acquired during the marriage by either spouse). If you are single, follow the "Common Law" rules below.

  - In Common Law States: All property in which your name is on the title document, unless it is held as "joint tenants" or "tenants-by-the-entireties" and all other property which you own, earned or purchased in your own name. Please check the Appendix for information relating to the spouse's minimum statutory share of an estate.

CHAPTER 3

Steps In Preparing Your Own Will

There are several steps that must be followed to properly prepare your Will using this book. None of them are very difficult or overly complicated. However, they must be done carefully in order to effectively accomplish what you set out to do -- be assured that your property is left to those loved ones that you choose and that your loved ones are properly cared for after your death.

This chapter will briefly outline the necessary steps which must be followed to prepare a valid Will with this book. You will probably refer back to this chapter several times in the course of preparing your own Will to be certain that you are on the right track and have not left out any steps.

The following steps are numbered 1 through 10 for your ease in following them:

Step #1:   Read through this entire book. You are advised to read carefully through this entire book before you actually begin preparing your own Will. By doing this you will gain an overview of the entire process and will have a much better idea of where you are heading before you actually begin the preparation of your Will.

Step #2:   Fill in the Personal Questionnaire contained in Chapter 4. This questionnaire is designed to compile all of the necessary personal information for your Will preparation. Information regarding your personal and business assets, percentages of ownership of these assets, marital relationship, names and addresses of relatives, and many other items will be gathered together in this questionnaire for your use. Refer to the information in Chapter 2, if necessary, to determine the correct amount of your property ownership in jointly-held assets.

Step #3:   Review your own state's legal requirements as contained in the Appendix. Although the standard Will clauses used in this book will alleviate most of the concerns raised by these legal requirements, there may be certain of your own state's requirements which will affect how you decide to prepare your own Will.

Step #4:   Read through all of the Will clauses contained in Chapter 5 and decide which ones you wish to include in your own Will. This is one of the most important steps in the process and one which must be done very carefully. The various clauses are, for the most part, self-explanatory and you will be able to easily decide which ones apply to your situation and should be included in your will. However, you are advised to read through each and every clause in Chapter 5 before you decide on the final choices for your own Will.

Step #5:   Make a photo-copy of all of those portions of Chapter 5 which will be included in your own Will, including the mandatory clauses as noted. After you have done this, number each included clause consecutively beginning with #1.

Step #6:   Type a clean original of your Will. With your filled-in photo-copied version before you, this should be a relatively easy task of simply copying the provisions which you have selected.

Step #7:   Proofread your entire Will very carefully to be certain that it is exactly what you want. If there are any typographical errors or if you want to change some provision, no matter how slight--you MUST retype that page of your Will.

Step #8: Assemble your witnesses and notary public and formally sign your Will. This is known as the *Execution* of your Will and must be done very carefully following the details contained in Chapter 8.

Step #9: Make a photo-copy of your Will and give it to the Executor that you have named in your Will. Store the original of your Will in a safe place as outlined in Chapter 8.

Step #10: Review your Will periodically and prepare a new Will or *Codicil* (a formally-executed change to a Will) if necessary as detailed in Chapter 9.

That's all there is to it. Actually, that may sound like a lot of work and bother, but realize that you would have to follow many of the same steps even if a lawyer were to prepare your Will. However, in that case, you would give him or her all of the information and he or she would simply prepare a Will in much the same fashion that you will use in this book. The difference, of course, is that you must pay an often exorbitant price to have this done by a lawyer. Additionally, by preparing your Will yourself and doing so at your own pace, you are certain to take more care and give more thought to the entire process than if you have someone else prepare it for you.

The following is a Checklist of the 10 steps noted above:

1. Read this entire book first.

2. Fill in the Personal Questionnaire.

3. Review your state's legal requirements.

4. Choose the Will clauses for your Will.

5. Make a photo-copy rough-draft version of your Will.

6. Type an original of your Will.

7.   Carefully proofread your Will.

8.   Assemble the witnesses and notary public and sign your Will.

9.   Give a copy of your Will to your Executor and store the original in a safe place.

10.   Review your Will periodically and make any changes in a formal manner.

CHAPTER 4

Personal Questionnaire

Before you begin to actually prepare your own Will, you must understand what your assets are, who your beneficiaries are to be and what your personal desires are as to how those assets should be distributed among your beneficiaries.

Since you may only give away property which you actually own, before you prepare your Will it is helpful to gather all of the information regarding your personal financial situation together in one place. Part 1 of this Questionnaire will assist you in that task. If you have any questions relating to ownership of these assets, (For example: Is the property held in "joint tenancy"?), please refer back to the discussion in Chapter 2.

Determining who your dependents are, what their financial circumstances are, what gifts you wish to leave them, and whether you wish to make other persons or organizations beneficiaries under your Will are questions that will be answered as you complete Part 2 of the following Questionnaire.

Together, these two Parts of the Questionnaire should provide you with all of the necessary information to make the actual preparation of your Will a relatively easy task. In addition, the actual process of filling out these questions will gently force you to think about and make the important decisions which must be made in the planning and preparation of your Will.

When you have finished completing this Questionnaire, have it before you as you select and fill in your personal Will clauses in the next chapter.

It may also be prudent to leave a photo-copy of this Questionnaire with the original of your Will, in order to provide a readily-accessible inventory of your assets and list of your beneficiaries for use by your Executor in managing your estate.

PART 1

NET WORTH OF YOUR ESTATE

What Are Your Assets?

CASH AND BANK ACCOUNTS

Checking Account ....$ _____

       Bank _____

       Account # _____

Savings Account...$ _____

       Bank _____

       Account # _____

Certificate of Deposit ....$ _____

       Held by _____

       Expiration date _____

Certificate of Deposit ....$ _____

       Held by _____

       Expiration date _____

Other Account .... $ _____

    Bank _____

    Account # _____

Total Cash .... $ _____

LIFE INSURANCE AND ANNUITY CONTRACTS
(Can not be left by Will)

Ordinary Life.. $ _____

    Company _____

    Policy # _____

    Beneficiary _____

Endowment .... $ _____

    Company _____

    Policy # _____

    Beneficiary _____

Term... $ _____

    Company _____

    Policy # _____

    Beneficiary _____

Annuity Contract .... $ _____

        Company _____

        Contract # _____

        Beneficiary _____

Total Insurance .... $ _____

ACCOUNTS AND NOTES RECEIVABLE
(Debts payable to you)

Accounts .... $ _____

        Due from _____

Notes .... $ _____

        Due from _____

Other Debts .... $ _____

        Due from _____

Other Debts .... $ _____

        Due from _____

Other Debts .... $ _____

        Due from _____

Total Accounts & Notes .... $ _____

STOCKS

Company _____

    # and Type of shares _____

    Value.. $ _____

Company _____

    # and Type of shares _____

    Value.. $ _____

Company _____

    # and Type of shares _____

    Value.. $ _____

Company _____

    # and Type of shares _____

    Value.. $ _____

Company _____

    # and Type of shares _____

    Value.. $ _____

Company _____

    # and Type of shares _____

    Value.. $ _____

Total Stocks.. $ _____

BONDS

Company _____

     # and Type of shares _____

     Value.. $ _____

Company _____

     # and Type of shares _____

     Value.. $ _____

Company _____

     # and Type of shares _____

     Value.. $ _____

Company _____

     # and Type of shares _____

     Value.. $ _____

Company _____

     # and Type of shares _____

     Value.. $ _____

Company _____

     # and Type of shares _____

     Value.. $ _____

Total Bonds .... $ _____

BUSINESS INTERESTS

Individual Proprietorship

Name _____

Your net value .... $ _____

Interest in Partnership

Name _____

Gross value $_____

Percentage Interest _____

Your net value .... $ _____

Close Corporation Interest

Name _____

Gross value $_____

Percentage shares held _____

Your net value .... $ _____

Total Business Value .... $ _____

EMPLOYEE BENEFIT AND PENSION/PROFIT-SHARING PLANS
(Can not be left by Will)

Company _____

    Net Value.. $ _____

Company _____

    Net Value.. $ _____

Company _____

    Net Value.. $ _____

Total Benefit Value .... $ _____

REAL ESTATE
(Property held in Joint Tenancy or Tenancy by Entireity may not be passed on through the use of a Will)

Residence

    Location _____

    Value: $ _____

    How held and Percent held? (Joint Tenants, Tenancy in Common, etc?)

    _____/_____%

    Value your share .... $ _____

Vacation Home

    Location _____

        Value: $ _____

        How held and Percent held? (Joint Tenants, Tenancy in Common, etc?)

        _____/_____%

        Value your share... $ _____

Vacant Land

    Location _____

        Value: $ _____

        How held and Percent held? (Joint Tenants, Tenancy in Common, etc?)

        _____/_____%

        Value your share... $ _____

Income property

    Location _____

        Value: $ _____

        How held and Percent held? (Joint Tenants, Tenancy in Common, etc?)

        _____/_____%

        Value your share....................................... $ _____

Total Real Estate... $ _____

PERSONAL PROPERTY

Car.. $ _____

Car.. $ _____

Boat/other vehicles .... $ _____

Household furnishings... $ _____

Jewelry and furs... $ _____

Art work .... $ _____

Total Personal Property .... $ _____

MISCELLANEOUS ASSETS

Royalties, Patents, Copyrights .... $ _____

Other... $ _____

Other... $ _____

Other... $ _____

Other... $ _____

Total Miscellaneous... $ _____

TOTAL ASSETS

Cash Total .... $ _____

Life Insurance Total .... $ _____

Accounts & Notes Total .... $ _____

Stocks Total .... $ _____

Bonds Total .... $ _____

Business Total .... $ _____

Pension Total .... $ _____

Real Estate Total .... $ _____

Personal Property Total .... $ _____

Miscellaneous Total .... $ _____

TOTAL ASSETS .... $ _____

WHAT ARE YOUR LIABILITIES?

NOTES AND LOANS PAYABLE
(Debts owed to others)

Payable to _____

Amount Due .... $ _____

Payable to _____

    Amount Due .... $ _____

ACCOUNTS PAYABLE

Payable to _____

    Amount Due .... $ _____

Payable to _____

    Amount Due .... $ _____

MORTGAGES PAYABLE

Property location _____

    Payable to _____

    Amount Due .... $ _____

Property location _____

    Payable to _____

    Amount Due .... $ _____

TAXES DUE

    Income .... $ _____

    Property .... $ _____

MISCELLANEOUS LIABILITIES

To Whom Due _____

    Amount Due .... $ _____

To Whom Due _____

    Amount Due .... $ _____

To Whom Due _____

    Amount Due .... $ _____

TOTAL LIABILITIES

    Total Loans Payable .... $ _____

    Total Accounts Payable .... $ _____

    Total Mortgages Payable .... $ _____

    Total Taxes Payable .... $ _____

    Total Miscellaneous .... $ _____

TOTAL LIABILITIES .... $ _____

WHAT IS YOUR NET WORTH?

TOTAL ASSETS.. $ _____

....minus (-)

TOTAL LIABILITIES.. $ _____

....equals (=)

YOUR TOTAL NET WORTH....................................... $ _____

IMPORTANT PAPERS LOCATION

Safe Deposit Box Location _____

Box Number _____

Key Location _____

Location of other important papers _____

PART 2

BENEFICIARIES OF YOUR ESTATE

Who are your Dependents?

SPOUSE _____

Maiden Name _____

Date of Marriage _____

Date of Birth _____

Address _____

_____

Current Income $ _____

AMOUNT, SPECIFIC ITEMS, OR SHARE OF ESTATE

WHICH YOU DESIRE TO LEAVE _____

_____

_____

CHILDREN _____

Date of Birth _____

Address _____

_____

Spouse's Name (if any) _____

Current Income $ _____

AMOUNT, SPECIFIC ITEMS, OR SHARE OF ESTATE

WHICH YOU DESIRE TO LEAVE _____

_____

_____

CHILDREN _____

Date of Birth _____

Address _____

_____

Spouse's Name (if any) _____

Current Income $ _____

AMOUNT, SPECIFIC ITEMS, OR SHARE OF ESTATE

WHICH YOU DESIRE TO LEAVE _____

_____

CHILDREN _____

Date of Birth _____

Address _____

_____

Spouse's Name (if any) _____

Current Income $ _____

AMOUNT, SPECIFIC ITEMS, OR SHARE OF ESTATE

WHICH YOU DESIRE TO LEAVE _____

_____

_____

CHILDREN _____

Date of Birth _____

Address _____

_____

Spouse's Name (if any) _____

Current Income $ _____

AMOUNT, SPECIFIC ITEMS, OR SHARE OF ESTATE

WHICH YOU DESIRE TO LEAVE _____

_____

GRANDCHILDREN _____

Date of Birth _____

Address _____

_____

Current Income $ _____

AMOUNT, SPECIFIC ITEMS, OR SHARE OF ESTATE

WHICH YOU DESIRE TO LEAVE _____

_____

_____

GRANDCHILDREN _____

Date of Birth _____

Address _____

_____

Current Income $ _____

AMOUNT, SPECIFIC ITEMS, OR SHARE OF ESTATE

WHICH YOU DESIRE TO LEAVE _____

_____

_____

GRANDCHILDREN _____

Date of Birth _____

Address _____

_____

Current Income $ _____

AMOUNT, SPECIFIC ITEMS, OR SHARE OF ESTATE

WHICH YOU DESIRE TO LEAVE _____

_____

_____

GRANDCHILDREN _____

Date of Birth _____

Address _____

_____

Current Income $ _____

AMOUNT, SPECIFIC ITEMS, OR SHARE OF ESTATE

WHICH YOU DESIRE TO LEAVE _____

_____

_____

PARENT _____

Date of Birth _____

Address _____

_____

Current Income $ _____

AMOUNT, SPECIFIC ITEMS, OR SHARE OF ESTATE

WHICH YOU DESIRE TO LEAVE _____

_____

_____

PARENT _____

Date of Birth _____

Address _____

_____

Current Income $ _____

AMOUNT, SPECIFIC ITEMS, OR SHARE OF ESTATE

WHICH YOU DESIRE TO LEAVE _____

_____

_____

OTHER DEPENDENT _____

Date of Birth _____

Address _____

_____

Current Income _____

AMOUNT, SPECIFIC ITEMS, OR SHARE OF ESTATE

WHICH YOU DESIRE TO LEAVE _____

_____

_____

Any other relatives, friends, or organizations
that you wish to leave gifts to?

NAME _____

Relationship _____

Address _____

_____

AMOUNT, SPECIFIC ITEMS, OR SHARE OF ESTATE

WHICH YOU DESIRE TO LEAVE _____

_____

_____

NAME _____

Relationship _____

Address _____

_____

AMOUNT, SPECIFIC ITEMS, OR SHARE OF ESTATE

WHICH YOU DESIRE TO LEAVE _____

_____

_____

NAME _____

Relationship _____

Address _____

_____

AMOUNT, SPECIFIC ITEMS, OR SHARE OF ESTATE

WHICH YOU DESIRE TO LEAVE _____

_____

_____

Any persons whom you wish to specifically leave out of your Will?

NAME _____

Relationship _____

Address _____

_____

NAME _____

Relationship _____

Address _____

_____

NAME _____

Relationship _____

Address _____

_____

CHAPTER 5

Will Clauses

This chapter contains a listing of all of the necessary Will clauses which you will need to complete your own Will. Although not every possible contingency is covered by these clauses, most choices for dispositions under your Will should be covered by the clauses shown in this chapter. By using the clauses contained in this Chapter you will be able to prepare a Will in which you may:

- Make specific gifts of cash to anyone;

- Make specific gifts of personal property to anyone;

- Make specific gifts of real estate to anyone;

- Make specific gifts of certain shares of your estate;

- Disinherit anyone from receiving anything from your estate;

- Make a gift of the rest (*residue*) of your assets to anyone;

- Choose an Executor to administer your estate;

- Choose a Guardian for any minor children;

- Set up a Trust and choose a Trustee for children's gifts;

- Declare your intention to be an organ donor;

- Declare your choice for funeral/cremation arrangements.

Please note that there are certain clauses which are mandatory for all Wills and you must include these clauses in your own Will. These mandatory clauses are clearly marked for your ease in preparing your Will. In choosing your own individual clauses, simply follow the directions and instructions which are given immediately prior to each specific clause and fill in the appropriate blanks.

As you are choosing and preparing your specific Will clauses, it is suggested that you have before you the completed Personal Questionnaire from Chapter 4. The information which you compiled for that questionnaire will be your guide for preparing your Will, both in terms of being certain that you have disposed of all of your assets and in terms of being certain that you have left gifts to all those persons or organizations that you wished to.

When you have completed your selection of clauses, read through them carefully to be sure that you have filled in the blanks exactly to your wishes. Then, read through the sample Will contained in the next Chapter to see how a completed Will is arranged. Then turn to Chapter 7 for instructions on typing and preparing your Will for signature.

WILL CLAUSES

TITLE--MANDATORY: the below title is mandatory for all Wills and must be included. Fill in the name blank with your full legal name. If you have been known under more than one name, use your principal name. Do not number this title.

LAST WILL AND TESTAMENT OF [*your full name*] _____

IDENTIFICATION CLAUSE--MANDATORY: This clause must be included in all Wills. Do not number this clause. In the first blank, include any other names which you are known by. Do this by adding the phrase: "also known as" after your principal full name. For example: John James Smith, also known as Jimmy John Smith. In the spaces provided for your residence, use the location of your principal residence; where you live permanently.

I, [*your full name and any other names you have used*] _____,
a resident of [*name of city or town*] _____, [*name of county*]
_____, [*name of state*] _____, declare that this is my
Last Will and Testament and I revoke all previous Wills and codicils.

MARITAL STATUS CLAUSE--MANDATORY if you are unmarried and have no children. If used, number this clause #1 in the box.

☐   I have never been married and I have no children.

MARITAL STATUS CLAUSE--MANDATORY if you are currently married. If used, number this clause #1 in the box.

☐   I am married to [*spouse's full name*] _____.

MARITAL STATUS CLAUSE--MANDATORY if you have been previously married. If you use this clause, number it consecutively.

☐ I was previously married to [*previous spouse's full name, if any*] _____. That marriage ended in [*year*] _____ by [*divorce, death, annulment*] _____.

CHILDREN IDENTIFICATION CLAUSE--MANDATORY if you have any children who are living. If you need more spaces than are shown, simply repeat the information. Then number this clause consecutively.

☐ I have [*number*] _____ children living. Their names, addresses and dates of birth are:

[*child's name*] _____

[*child's address*] _____

[*child's date of birth*] _____

[*child's name*] _____

[*child's address*] _____

[*child's date of birth*] _____

[*child's name*] _____

[*child's address*] _____

[*child's date of birth*] _____

[child's name] _____

[child's address] _____

[child's date of birth] _____

[child's name] _____

[child's address] _____

[child's date of birth] _____

[child's name] _____

[child's address] _____

[child's date of birth] _____

[child's name] _____

[child's address] _____

[child's date of birth] _____

[child's name] _____

[child's address] _____

[child's date of birth] _____

GRANDCHILDREN IDENTIFICATION CLAUSE--MANDATORY if you have any grandchildren living. Number it consecutively.

☐   I have [*number*] _____ grandchildren living. Their names, addresses and dates of birth are:

[*grandchild's name*] _____

[*grandchild's address*] _____

[*grandchild's date of birth*] _____

[*grandchild's name*] _____

[*grandchild's address*] _____

[*grandchild's date of birth*] _____

[*grandchild's name*] _____

[*grandchild's address*] _____

[*grandchild's date of birth*] _____

[*grandchild's name*] _____

[*grandchild's address*] _____

[*grandchild's date of birth*] _____

[*grandchild's name*] _____

[*grandchild's address*] _____

[*grandchild's date of birth*] _____

[grandchild's name] _____

[grandchild's address] _____

[grandchild's date of birth] _____

[grandchild's name] _____

[grandchild's address] _____

[grandchild's date of birth] _____

ENTIRE ESTATE GIFT CLAUSE--OPTIONAL: Use this clause if you are leaving all of your property to one person or organization. Where you are asked to state the beneficiary's relationship, simply state their kinship, (For example: my mother), their status as a friend or co-worker, or the status as an organization (For example: my church or my alma mater). If you use this clause, do not use any other clause which leaves a gift to another person or organization.

If you desire to leave portions of your estate to more than one person, use the "Specific Gift" clauses that follow. Your choice for alternate beneficiary may be one or more persons. It is recommended to always specifically name your beneficiary(s), rather than use a description only, such as "my children". Number this clause consecutively.

☐ I give my entire estate to *[relationship]* _____ , *[beneficiary's full name]* _____ , or if not surviving, to *[relationship]* _____ , *[alternate beneficiary's full name]* _____ .

SPECIFIC GIFTS CLAUSE--OPTIONAL: Use the following line and the paragraphs that follow as one clause. Number the entire clause consecutively. Use as many of the "I give . . ." paragraphs as is necessary to complete your chosen gifts. In these paragraphs, you may make any type of gift that you wish, either a cash gift, a gift of a specific piece of personal property or real estate or a specific share of your total estate. If you wish to give some of your estate in the form of portions of the total, it is recommended to use fractional portions. For example, if you wish to leave your estate in equal shares to two persons, use "I give one-half of my total estate to . . . " for each party.

In your description of the property, you should be as specific and precise as possible. For land, it is suggested that you use the description exactly as shown on the Deed. For personal property, be certain that your description clearly differentiates your gift from any other property. For example: "I give my blue velvet coat which was a gift from my brother John to . . . "

The choice of alternate beneficiary is for the purpose of allowing you to designate someone to receive the gift if your first choice dies before you do. Your alternate beneficiary may be one or more persons or organizations. Or, you may delete the alternate beneficiary choice and substitute "the residue". Doing so will cause the gift to pass under your "residuary clause", which is discussed later in this chapter.

☐   I make the following specific gifts:

I give [complete description of property] _____ to [relationship] _____, [beneficiary's full name] _____, or, if not surviving, to [relationship and full name of alternate beneficiary OR "the residue"] _____.

I give [complete description of property] _____ to [relationship] _____, [beneficiary's full name] _____, or, if not surviving, to [relationship and full name of alternate beneficiary OR "the residue"] _____.

I give [*complete description of property*] _____ to
[*relationship*] _____, [*beneficiary's full name*]
_____, or, if not surviving, to [*relationship and full
name of alternate beneficiary OR "the residue"*]
_____.

I give [*complete description of property*] _____ to
[*relationship*] _____, [*beneficiary's full name*]
_____, or, if not surviving, to [*relationship and full
name of alternate beneficiary OR "the residue"*]
_____.

I give [*complete description of property*] _____ to
[*relationship*] _____, [*beneficiary's full name*]
_____, or, if not surviving, to [*relationship and full
name of alternate beneficiary OR "the residue"*]
_____.

I give [*complete description of property*] _____ to
[*relationship*] _____, [*beneficiary's full name*]
_____, or, if not surviving, to [*relationship and full
name of alternate beneficiary OR "the residue"*]
_____.

I give [*complete description of property*] _____ to
[*relationship*] _____, [*beneficiary's full name*]
_____, or, if not surviving, to [*relationship and full
name of alternate beneficiary OR "the residue"*]
_____.

RESIDUARY CLAUSE--MANDATORY: This clause must be included in every will. It should be numbered consecutively. With it, you will choose the person, persons, or organization to receive anything not covered by other terms of your Will. Even if you feel that you have given away everything that you own under other terms of your Will, this can be a very important clause, if, for any reason, other gifts under your Will are not completed. For example, if a beneficiary refuses to accept your gift or the chosen beneficiary has died and no alternate was selected or both the beneficiary and alternate has died, the gift is put back into your estate and would pass under the "residuary clause". If there is no "residuary clause", any property not disposed of under your Will is treated as if you did not have a Will. To avoid this, it is strongly recommended that you make this clause mandatory.

☐ I give all the rest of my property, whether real or personal, wherever located, to [relationship] _____, [beneficiary's full name] _____, or, if not surviving, to [relationship] _____, [full name of alternate beneficiary] _____.

DEBT FORGIVENESS CLAUSE--OPTIONAL: you may use this clause to forgive any debts owed to you personally. If used, number this clause consecutively.

☐ I forgive the following debt(s) owed to me:

[description of debt] _____
[full name of debtor] _____.

[description of debt] _____
[full name of debtor] _____.

SURVIVORSHIP CLAUSE--MANDATORY: this clause should be included in every Will. Number it consecutively. This provides for a period of survival for any beneficiary. The practical effect of this is to be certain that your property passes under your Will and not that of a beneficiary who dies shortly after receiving your gift.

☐ All beneficiaries named in this Will must survive me by thirty days to receive any gift under this Will. If any beneficiary and I should die simultaneously, I shall be conclusively presumed to have survived that beneficiary for purposes of this Will.

DISINHERITANCE CLAUSE--OPTIONAL: use this clause to specifically disinherit anyone from receiving property under your Will. It is much safer to specifically name the person to be disinherited than to simply rely upon their non-mention in the Will. To disinherit children and grandchildren of deceased children, they must be mentioned specifically. In the case of children born after a Will is executed and of spouses of a marriage which takes place after a Will is executed, there are differing provisions in many states as to the effect of their not being mentioned in a Will. Please see the Appendix for information as to your particular state. The safest method, however, is to specifically mention anyone to be disinherited and, also, to review your Will each time there is a change in your family circumstances. Please see Chapter 9.

☐ I specifically disinherit [*relationship*] _____, [*full name and address of person to be disinherited*] _____ and any other person not specifically named as a beneficiary in this Will.

EXECUTOR CLAUSE--MANDATORY: With this clause, you will make your choice of Executor, the person who will administer your estate and an alternate choice if your first choice is unable to serve. A spouse, sibling, or other trusted party is usually chosen to act as executor. The person chosen should be a resident of your home state. Additionally, you grant the executor broad power to manage your estate and also provide that he or she not be required to post a bond in order to be appointed. Number this clause consecutively.

> ☐ I appoint *[relationship]* _____, *[full name of Executor]* _____ as Executor, to serve without bond. If not surviving or otherwise unable to serve, I appoint *[relationship]* _____, *[full name of alternate Executor]* _____ as alternate Executor, also to serve without bond. In addition to any powers, authority and discretion granted by law, I grant such Executor or alternate Executor full power to perform any acts, in his or her sole discretion and without court approval, for the management and distribution of my estate.

GUARDIANSHIP CLAUSE--OPTIONAL: with this clause you may designate your choice as to whom you wish to care for any of your minor children after you are gone. If you are married, your present spouse is generally appointed, regardless of your designation in a Will. However, even if you are married, it is a good idea to choose your spouse as first choice and then provide a second choice. This will cover the contingency in which both you and your spouse die in a single accident.

Your choice should obviously be a trusted person whom you feel would provide the best care for your children in your absence. Be aware, however, that the court is guided, but not bound, by this particular choice in your Will, The court's decision in appointing a child's guardian is based upon what would be in the best interests of the child. Additionally, you grant the guardian broad power to care for and manage your children's property and also provide that he or she not be required to post a bond in order to be appointed. If used, number this clause consecutively.

☐ If a Guardian is needed for any of my minor children, I appoint [*relationship*] _____, [*full name of Guardian*] _____ as Guardian of the person(s) and property of my minor children, to serve without bond. If not surviving or otherwise unable to serve, I appoint [*relationship*] _____, [*full name of alternate Guardian*] _____ as alternate Guardian, also to serve without bond. In addition to any powers, authority and discretion granted by law, I grant such Guardian or alternate Guardian full power to perform any acts, in his or her sole discretion and without court approval, for the management and distribution of the property of my minor children.

CHILDREN'S TRUST FUND CLAUSE--OPTIONAL: it is with this clause that you may set up a Trust Fund for any of your minor children. You also may delay the time when they will actually have unfettered control over your gift. It is not recommended, however, to attempt to delay receipt of control beyond the age of 30.

The choice of trustee is generally a spouse if alive, with the alternate being a trusted friend or family member. The terms of the trust provide that the trustee may distribute any or all of the income or principal to the children as he or she deems necessary to provide for their health, support, and education. The trust will terminate when either the specific age is reached, the money is spent prior to that age, or the child dies prematurely. Additionally, you grant the trustee broad power to manage the trust and also provide that he or she not be required to post a bond in order to be appointed. Number this entire clause consecutively.

☐ If any of my children are under [*21. 25, or 30 years of age*] _____ on my death, I direct that any property that I give them under this Will be held in an individual trust for each child, under the following terms, until each shall reach [*21, 25, or 30 years of age*] _____.

A. I appoint [*relationship*] _____, [*full name of trustee*] _____ as trustee of any and all required trusts, to serve without bond. If not surviving or otherwise unable to serve, then I appoint [*relationship*] _____, [*full name of alternate trustee*] _____ as alternate Trustee, also to serve without bond. In addition to all powers, authority and discretion -granted by law, I grant such trustee or alternate trustee full power to perform any act, in his or her sole discretion and without court approval, to distribute and manage the assets of any such trust.

B. In the trustee's sole discretion, the trustee may distribute any or all of the principal, income or both as deemed necessary for the beneficiary's health, support, welfare and education. Any income not distributed shall be added to the trust principal.

C. Any such trust shall terminate when the beneficiary reaches the required age, when the beneficiary dies prior to reaching the required age, or when all trust funds have been distributed . Upon termination, any remaining undistributed principal and income shall pass to the beneficiary, or if not surviving, to the beneficiary's heirs.

ORGAN DONATION CLAUSE--OPTIONAL: use this clause to provide for any use of your body after death. You may, if you so desire, limit your donation to certain parts, for example, your eyes. If so desired, simply delete "any of my body parts and/or organs" from the following provision and insert your chosen donation. If used, number this clause consecutively.

☐ I declare that, pursuant to the Uniform Anatomical Gift Act, I donate any of my body parts and/or organs to any medical institution willing to accept them, and I direct my executor to carry out such donation.

FUNERAL ARRANGEMENTS CLAUSE --OPTIONAL: use this clause to make known your wishes as to funeral arrangements. It is also a good idea to leave information regarding these desires with your spouse or a close friend or relative, in as much as it may be difficult to obtain your Will quickly in an emergency. Number this clause consecutively.

☐ Funeral arrangements have been made with [*name and address of funeral service*] _____ for burial at [*name of cemetery*] _____ and I direct my Executor to carry out such arrangements.

CREMATION ARRANGEMENTS CLAUSE--OPTIONAL: use this clause to make known your wishes as to any cremation arrangements. It is also a good idea to leave information regarding these desires with your spouse or a close friend or relative, in as much as it may be difficult to obtain your Will quickly in an emergency. Number this clause consecutively.

☐ Cremation arrangements have been made with [*name and address of crematorium*] _____, and I direct my Executor to carry out such arrangements.

SIGNATURE AND WITNESS CLAUSES--MANDATORY: all of the following remaining portions of your Will are mandatory and must be included in your Will. Do not number any of these provisions. You will fill in the number of pages and the appropriate dates after you have properly typed or had your Will typed.

I publish and sign this Last Will and Testament, consisting of [number] _____ typewritten pages, on [month, date and year] _____, and declare that I do so freely, for the purposes expressed, under no constraint or undue influence, and that I am of sound mind and of legal age.

[signature of Testator] _____
[typewritten name of Testator] _____

On [month, date, and year] _____, in the presence of all of us, the above-named testator published and signed this Last Will and Testament, and then at testator's request, and in testator's presence, and in each other's presence, we all signed below as witnesses, and we declare, under penalty of perjury, that, to the best of our knowledge, the testator signed this instrument freely, under no constraint or undue influence, and is of sound mind and legal age.

[signature of Witness] _____
[typewritten name of Witness]_____
[address of Witness] _____

[signature of Witness] _____
[typewritten name of Witness]_____
[address of Witness] _____

[signature of Witness] _____
[typewritten name of Witness]_____
[address of Witness] _____

SELF-PROVING AFFIDAVIT--MANDATORY: prepare and use this Affidavit with all Wills. Although a few states have not enacted legislation to allow for their use in court, the current trend is for all courts to allow their use. This Affidavit will allow for your signature on your Will to be proved without the necessity of having the three witnesses appear in court, a point which will save time, money and trouble in having your Will admitted to probate.

SELF-PROVING AFFIDAVIT

We, the undersigned testator and witnesses, being first sworn on oath, state that, in the presence of all the witnesses, the testator published and signed the above Last Will and Testament and then, at testator's request, and in the presence of the testator and of each other, each of the witnesses signed as witnesses, and that, to the best of our knowledge, the testator signed said Last Will and Testament freely, under no constraint or undue influence, and is of sound mind and legal age.

[*signature of Testator*] _____

[*typewritten name of Testator*] _____

[*signature of Witness*] _____

[*typewritten name of Witness*]_____

[*address of Witness*] _____

[*signature of Witness*] _____

[*typewritten name of Witness*]_____

[*address of Witness*] _____

[*signature of Witness*] _____

[*typewritten name of Witness*]_____

[*address of Witness*] _____

County of_____}   SS.
State of _____}

Subscribed, sworn to and acknowledged before me on [*month, date and year*] _____ by [*full name of testator*] _____, the testator, and by [*full name of first witness*] _____, [*full name of second witness*] _____, [*full name of third witness*] _____, the witnesses.

[*signature of Notary Public*] _____
[*typewritten name of Notary Public*] _____

Notary Public, in and for the
County of _____,
State of _____

CHAPTER 6

Sample Will

In this chapter, a complete sample Will is presented. It was prepared using the Will clauses contained in Chapter 5. By reviewing this sample Will, you will be able to see what a completed Will should look like and how the various parts are put together.

In this sample Will, a Mrs. Mary Smith is the fictional Testator. Mrs. Smith is married to Mr. John Smith, and they have two minor children who live with them. In her Will, Mrs. Smith wishes to accomplish the following:

- Leave her oval diamond necklace to a friend;

- Leave her brown mink coat to her mother;

- Leave $10,000 to each of her children, to be held in trust until they are 21;

- Leave all the rest of her estate to her husband;

- Appoint her husband to act as:

  - Executor of the Will;

  - Guardian of the children;

  - Trustee of the children's trust;

- Forgive a $1,000.00 debt owed by one of her sisters;

- Declare her intention to be an organ donor;

- Designate her intentions for funeral arrangements.

By filling in the appropriate blanks in the Will clauses, the fictional Mrs. Mary Smith is able to easily and quickly prepare a Will which accomplishes all of her desires. She may rest assured that, by having properly prepared and signed a Last Will and Testament, her wishes will be carried out on her death.

LAST WILL AND TESTAMENT OF MARY ELLEN SMITH

I, MARY ELLEN SMITH, a resident of the Town of Centerville, County of Washington and State of Illinois, declare that this is my Last Will and Testament and I revoke all previous Wills and Codicils.

1.   I am married to JOHN ALAN SMITH.

2.   I was previously married to Robert David Jones. That marriage ended in 1980 by divorce.

3.   I have 2 (two) children living. Their names, addresses and dates of birth are:

ALICE MARY SMITH, 16 Main Street, Centerville, Illinois
April 21, 1984

JAMES JOHN SMITH, 16 Main Street, Centerville, Illinois
October 26, 1987

4.   I make the following specific gifts:

I give my Tiffany Oval Diamond and Gold Necklace to my good friend, Susie Mitchell, of Hilltown, Indiana, or, if not surviving, to the residue.

I give my Brown Mink Coat, which was a gift from my husband, to my mother, Mrs. Mary Stuart of Naples, Florida, or, if not surviving, to my husband, John Alan Smith..

I give Ten Thousand Dollars, cash, ($10,000.00) to my daughter, Alice Mary Smith.

I give Ten Thousand Dollars, cash, ($10,000.00) to my son, James John Smith.

5.   I give all the rest of my property, whether real or personal, wherever located, to my husband, John Alan Smith, or, if not surviving, to my children, Alice Mary Smith and James John Smith, in equal shares.

6. I forgive the following debt owed to me: One Thousand Dollars ($1,000.00) due from my sister, Jane Smith, of New York, New York.

7. All beneficiaries named in this Will must survive me by thirty days to receive any gift under this Will. If any beneficiary and I should die simultaneously, I shall be conclusively presumed to have survived that beneficiary for purposes of this Will.

8. I specifically disinherit anyone not named as a beneficiary in this Will.

9. I appoint my husband, John Alan Smith, as Executor, to serve without bond. If not surviving or otherwise unable to serve, I appoint my brother, Harold Stuart, of Chicago, Illinois, as alternate Executor, also to serve without bond. In addition to any powers, authority and discretion granted by law, I grant my Executor or my alternate Executor full power to perform any acts, in his or her sole discretion and without court approval, for the management and distribution of my estate.

10. If a Guardian is needed for any of my minor children, I appoint my husband, John Alan Smith, as Guardian of the person(s) and property of my minor children, to serve without bond. If not surviving or otherwise unable to serve, I appoint my sister, Sally Stuart Hall, of Des Moines, Iowa, as alternate Guardian, also to serve without bond. In addition to any powers, authority and discretion granted by law, I grant such Guardian or alternate Guardian full power to perform any acts, in his or her sole discretion and without court approval, for the management and distribution of the property of my minor children.

11. If any of my children are under the age of 21 on my death, I direct that any property that I give them under this Will be held in an individual trust for each child, under the following terms, until each shall reach 21 years of age.

    A. I appoint, my husband, John Alan Smith, as trustee of any and all required trusts, to serve without bond. If not surviving or otherwise unable to serve, then I appoint my sister, Sally Stuart Hall, as alternate Trustee, also to serve without bond. In addition to all powers, authority and discretion granted by law, I grant the trustee or alternate trustee full power to perform any act, in his or her sole discretion and without court approval, to distribute and manage the assets of any such trust.

B. In the trustee's sole discretion, the trustee may distribute any or all of the principal, income or both as deemed necessary for the beneficiary's health, support, welfare and education. Any income not distributed shall be added to the trust principal.

C. Any such trust shall terminate when the beneficiary reaches the required age, when the beneficiary dies prior to reaching the required age, or when all trust funds have been distributed. Upon termination, remaining undistributed principal and income shall pass to the beneficiary, or if not surviving, to the beneficiary's heirs.

12. I declare that, pursuant to the Uniform Anatomical Gift Act, I wish to donate any of my body parts and/or organs to any medical institution willing to accept them, and I direct my Executor to carry out such donation.

13. I have made funeral arrangements with Centerville Funeral Parlor, Centerville, Illinois for burial at Shady Hill Cemetery, Centerville, Illinois, and I direct my Executor to carry out such arrangements.

I publish and sign this Last Will and Testament, consisting of 4 (four) typewritten pages, on January 1, 1988, and declare that I do so freely, for the purposes expressed, under no constraint or undue influence, and that I am of sound mind and of legal age.

MARY ELLEN SMITH
MARY ELLEN SMITH

On January 1, 1988, in the presence of all of us, the above-named testator published and signed this Last Will and Testament, and then, at testator's request, and in testator's presence, and in each other's presence, we all signed below as witnesses, and we declare, under penalty of perjury, that, to the best of our knowledge, the testator signed this instrument freely, under no constraint or undue influence, and is of sound mind and legal age.

JOAN ANDREWS, of Centerville, Illinois
JOAN ANDREWS

CHRISTOPHER WILLIAMS, of Centerville, Illinois
CHRISTOPHER WILLIAMS

SANDRA WRIGHT, of Centerville, Illinois
SANDRA WRIGHT

SELF-PROVING AFFIDAVIT

We, the undersigned testator and witnesses, being first sworn on oath, state that in the presence of all the witnesses, the testator published and signed the above Last Will and Testament and then, at testator's request and in the presence of the testator, and in each other's presence, each of the witnesses signed as witnesses, and that, to the best of our knowledge, the testator signed said Last Will and Testament freely, under no constraint or undue influence, and is of sound mind and legal age.

MARY ELLEN SMITH, testator, of Centerville, Illinois
MARY ELLEN SMITH

JOAN ANDREWS, witness, of Centerville, Illinois
JOAN ANDREWS

CHRISTOPHER WILLIAMS, witness, of Centerville, Illinois
CHRISTOPHER WILLIAMS

SANDRA WRIGHT, witness, of Centerville, Illinois
SANDRA WRIGHT

County of Washington } SS.
State of Illinois   }

Subscribed, sworn to and acknowledged before me on January 1, 1988, by MARY ELLEN SMITH, the testator, and JOAN ANDREWS, CHRISTOPHER WILLIAMS, and SANDRA WRIGHT, the witnesses.

ROBERT MERLIN   Notary Public,
ROBERT MERLIN   In and for the County of Washington ,
                     State of Illinois

CHAPTER 7

Preparing Your Will

This chapter will explain how to put your own Will together and properly type or have it typed and readied for your signature. Using your Personal Questionnaire as a guide, you should already have chosen your individual Will clauses from those contained in Chapter 5. You should also have reviewed the Sample Will contained in Chapter 6 for an example of what the completed Will should look like and how it should be arranged. [Note: At the end of this chapter are detailed instructions to be followed for preparing your Will if you are a resident of the State of Louisiana.]

As you have noted in the sample Will in the previous chapter, there is nothing very complicated about the arrangement of your Will. It is essentially a matter of combining all of the various clauses which you have already selected and filled in following the instructions in Chapter 5.

To make the preparation of your Will as easy as possible, it is recommended that you follow these steps:

1. Make a photo-copy of all of the clauses that you have selected for your own Will in Chapter 5. Don't forget to include all of those clauses which are indicated as "Mandatory". On your photo-copy

version, cross out all of the instructions and any other extraneous material which is not to become a part of your Will.

2. In consecutive order, number each clause of your Will in the boxes provided for that purpose at the beginning of each clause. Begin your numbering of clauses with the clause defining your marital status. End your numbering of clauses with the clause directly before the paragraph which begins: "I sign this Last Will and Testament, consisting of . . ."

3. When you have completed numbering your Will clauses, carefully re-read your entire Will to be certain that it is exactly as you wish.

4. After making any necessary changes, type yourself or have typed the entire Will on good quality typing paper. Type the "Self-Proving Affidavit" on a separate sheet of paper, as it is technically not a part of your Will, but rather a separate and distinct document.

5. After you have completed typing your Will, fill in the total number of pages in the Signature paragraph. Do not yet sign your Will or fill in the date in any of the spaces indicated.

6. Again, very carefully proofread your entire Will. Be certain that there are no errors. If there are any errors, re-type that particular page. DO NOT attempt to correct any errors with white-out type correcting fluid or with erasures of any kind. DO NOT cross-out or add anything to the typewritten words using a pen or pencil. Your Will, when completed properly, should look similar to the sample Will contained in the previous chapter, except that the signature and date spaces should be blank.

7. When you have a perfect original of your Will, with no corrections and no additions, staple all of the pages together in the top left hand corner. You are now ready to prepare for the *execution* (signing) of your Will. Please turn to the next chapter for instruction on signing your Will.

SPECIAL INSTRUCTIONS FOR RESIDENTS OF LOUISIANA

If you are a resident of Louisiana, the laws which govern your state are somewhat different than those of the other 49 states. The reason for this is that Louisiana law is derived from the French Civil Code rather than the English Common Law as are the other states. As such, there are slightly differing rules that must be followed in preparing a Will which is valid in the State of Louisiana.

Essentially, it is only the format of your Will which is changed for use in Louisiana. Please carefully follow the instructions below for the preparation of your Will for Louisiana. You should follow all of the steps outlined in Chapter 5 in choosing your personal Will clauses. However, as you are preparing your Will following the instructions in this chapter, you should make the following changes:

1.   After the title of your Will {for example: LAST WILL AND TESTAMENT OF [*your full name*] _____ } and before the first paragraph of your Will, correctly fill in the blanks and insert the following paragraph:

Before me, [*name of District Court Clerk*] _____, Clerk of the [*name of the District*] _____ District Court in and for the Parish of [*name of the Parish*] _____, being duly commissioned and qualified as such, and ex officio Notary Public, in the presence of 3 (three) competent witnesses residing in the Parish of [*name of Parish where witnesses reside*] _____, State of Louisiana, [*TESTATOR'S NAME*] _____, a resident of [*name of city or Parish where testator resides*] _____, State of Louisiana, personally came before me, the Notary, and declared to me, the Notary, in the presence of the undersigned witnesses that [*he or she*] _____ wished to make [*his or her*] _____ Last Will and Testament and that [*he or she*] _____ wished that I, the Notary, receive [*his or her*] _____ Last Will and Testament; and [*he or she*] _____ then dictated to me the following Last Will and Testament in the presence of the 3 (three) witnesses; and I, the Notary, received it from said dictation and wrote it down exactly as it was dictated to me in the presence of the testator and the 3 (three) witnesses, in the following words, to wit:

2.   At this point, as you are assembling your Will, you should insert your entire Will as prepared using Chapters 5 and 7, except do not use anything after the paragraph which begins: "I sign this Last Will and Testament, consisting of . . ."

Instead, fill in the correct insertions below and use the following at the end of your Will:

This Last Will and Testament of [TESTATOR'S NAME] _____ was dictated by the testator to me, the Notary, in the presence and hearing of the 3 (three) witnesses and was reduced to writing by me, the Notary, as dictated. I, the Notary, then read the above Last Will and Testament to the testator in the presence of the 3 (three) witnesses, and the testator, being satisfied with said Last Will and Testament then signed it in my presence and in the presence of the 3 (three) witnesses, and this all having been done, received, dictated, read, and signed at one time, without any interruption, and without turning aside to do any other act, in the Parish of [name of Parish] _____, State of Louisiana, on [month, date, and year] _____.

        [signature of Testator] _____
        [printed name of Testator] _____

        [signature of Notary Public] _____
        [printed name of Notary Public] _____

        Notary Public, in and for the
        Parish of _____,
        State of Louisiana.

On [month, date, and year] _____, in the presence of all of us, the above-named testator signed and declared to us that this is [his or her] _____ Last Will and Testament, and then at testator's request, and in [his or her] _____ presence, and in each other's presence, we all signed below as witnesses, and we declare, under penalty of perjury, that, to the best of our knowledge, the testator signed this instrument freely, under no constraint or undue influence, and is of sound mind and legal age.

[signature of Witness] _____
*[printed name of Witness]*_____
[address of Witness] _____

[signature of Witness] _____
*[printed name of Witness]*_____
[address of Witness] _____

[signature of Witness] _____
*[printed name of Witness]*_____
[address of Witness] _____

3. When you have assembled your entire Will and had it typewritten as indicated earlier in this Chapter for all Wills, you must go with your 3 (three) witnesses and take your Louisiana Will to the Clerk of the District Court for the Parish in which you reside. Request that the Clerk/Notary Public transcribe your Will exactly as you dictate it to him or her.

4. After you have dictated your Will to the Clerk and he or she has written it out, you, the Notary Public and the 3 (three) witnesses must sign the Will where indicated. You need not use the "Self-Proving Affidavit" shown at the end of Chapter 5 and you need not follow the steps outlined in Chapter 8 as they pertain to signing your Will. Once completed as outlined above, the written version of your Last Will and Testament is valid as a Will in the State of Louisiana.

CHAPTER 8

Signing Your Will

After you have successfully had your Will typed in the proper form, you are ready to sign it. DO NOT sign your Will until you have read this chapter and have all of the necessary witnesses and Notary Public present. The legal requirements of this chapter regarding the proper execution (signing) of your Will are extremely important and must not be deviated from in any manner for your Will to be legally valid. These requirements are not at all difficult to follow, but they must be followed precisely. It is these formal requirements that transform your Will from a mere piece of paper outlining your wishes to a legal document which grants the power to dispose of your property under court order after your death.

The reasons for the formality of these requirements are two-fold: first, by requiring a ceremonial-type signing of the document, it is hoped that the testator is made fully aware of the importance of what he or she is doing; and second, by requiring a formal signing witnessed by other adults, it is hoped that any instances of forgery, fraud, and coercion will be avoided, or at least lessened.

Again, these legal formalities must be observed strictly. DO NOT deviate from these instructions in any way. It is the formal execution or signing of your Will that makes it legally valid and failure to properly sign your Last

Will and Testament will render it invalid. To properly execute your Last Will and Testament, follow these few simple steps:

1. Select 3 (three) witnesses who will be available to assist you in witnessing your Will. These persons may be any adult who is not mentioned in the Will either as a beneficiary, executor, trustee, or guardian. They may be friends, neighbors, co-workers, even strangers. However, it is prudent to choose persons who have been stable members of your community, since they may be called upon to testify in court someday.

2. Arrange for all of your witnesses to meet you at the office or home of a local Notary Public. Many banks, real estate offices and government offices have notary services and most will be glad to assist you. (The Notary Public may NOT be one of the required three witnesses.)

3. In front of all of the witnesses and in front of the Notary Public, the following should take place in the order shown:

    A. You should state: "This is my Last Will and Testament, which I am about to sign. I ask that each of you witness my signature." There is no requirement that the witnesses know any of the terms of your Will or that they read any of your Will. All that is necessary is that they hear you state that it is your Will, that you request them to be witnesses, that they observe you sign your Will and that they also sign the Will in each other's presence.

    B. You will then sign your Will at the end, exactly as your name is typewritten on your Will, in the two (2) places indicated, in ink using a pen. Don't forget that one of your signatures will be on the "Self-Proving Affidavit".

    C. After you have signed, pass your Will to the first witness, who should sign in the two (2) places indicated and fill in his or her address.

D. After the first witness has signed, have the Will passed to the second Witness, who should also sign in the two (2) places indicated and fill in his or her address.

E. After the second witness has signed, have the Will passed to the third and final witness, who also signs in the two (2) places indicated and fills in his or her address. Throughout this ceremony, you and all of the witnesses must remain together. It is easier if you are all seated around a table or desk.

F. The final step is for the Notary Public to sign in the space indicated. When this step is completed, your Will is a valid legal document and you may be assured that your wishes will be carried out upon its presentation to a probate court on your death..

Please note that you should NEVER under any circumstances sign a duplicate of your Will. Once it has been properly executed following the steps above, you may make photo-copies of your Will. It is a good idea to label any of these as "COPIES".

Having completed your Will according to the foregoing instructions, it is now time to place your Will in a safe place. Many people keep their important papers in a safety deposit box at a local bank. Although this is an acceptable place for storing a Will, be advised that there are certain drawbacks. Your Will should be in a place which is readily accessible to your Executor at a moment's notice. Often there are certain unavoidable delays in gaining access to a safety deposit box in an emergency situation. If you are married, and your safety deposit box is jointly held, many of these delays can be avoided. If you decide to keep the original in your safe deposit box, it is a good idea to keep a clearly marked copy of your Will at home in a safe but easily located place, with a note as to where the original may be found.

An acceptable alternative to a safety deposit box is a home file box or desk that is used for home storage of your important papers. If possible, this storage place should be fireproof and under lock and key. Wherever you decide to store your Will, you will need to inform your chosen Executor of its location. The Executor will need to obtain the original of your Will shortly after your demise to determine if there are any necessary duties which must be looked after without delay, for example: funeral plans or organ donations.

It is also a good practice to store any life insurance policies and a copy of your birth certificate in the same location. Additionally, it is also prudent to store a copy of your Personal Questionnaire with your Will in order to provide your Executor with an inventory of your assets and a list of your heirs and beneficiaries. Any title documents or deeds relating to property which will be transferred under your Will may also be stored with your Will for the convenience of your Executor.

A final precaution is, if you desire, to allow the Executor whom you have named to keep a copy of your Will. Be careful, however, to be certain that you immediately inform him or her of any new Wills which you prepare or of any *Codicils* to your Will (formal changes to your Will) or of any decision to revoke your Will.

CHAPTER 9

Changing Your Will

In this chapter, instructions will be given on when and how to change your Will and how to revoke your Will. It is most important to follow these instructions carefully should you desire to make ANY changes to your Will. Failure to follow these instructions and an attempt to change your Will by such methods as crossing out a name or penciling in an addition could have the disastrous effect of voiding portions of your Will. Again, these instructions are not difficult to follow, but are very important to insure that your Will remains legally valid.

If you desire to totally revoke your Will, there are two acceptable methods:

- By signing a new Will which expressly states that you revoke all prior Wills. Wills prepared using this book will contain such a provision.

- By completely destroying, burning, or mutilating your Will, while it is in your possession if you actually intend that there be a revocation of your Will.

With respect to any changes which you may make in your Will at a later date, you should periodically review the provisions of your Will, keeping in mind the following:

- Changes in your personal wealth?

- Changes in your ownership of any property mentioned in your Will;

- The death or disfavor of any of the beneficiaries named in your Will;

- If the person whom you named as Executor, Guardian or Trustee in your Will is no longer able to serve;

- If you change the state of your residence;

- Whether you have been married since the date of your Will?

- Whether you have been divorced since the date of your Will?

- Whether you have had any children since the date of your Will?

- Whether you have adopted any children since the date of your Will?

- Whether you simply wish to make any corrections, deletions, or additions to any provisions in your Will?

If any of these matters apply, you will need to change your Will accordingly. Although it is possible to completely re-write your Will to take account of any of these changes, an easier method is to prepare and formally execute a Codicil, or a written change to a Will. Please bear in mind that all of the formalities surrounding the signing of your original Will must again be followed for any such changes contained in a Codicil to your Will to be valid.

Never attempt to change any portions of your Will by any other method. For example, DO NOT attempt to add provisions in the margin of your Will, either by typing them in or by writing them in. DO NOT attempt to cross-out any portions of your Will. These methods are not acceptable methods for the alteration of a Will, and could subject your Will to a court battle to determine its subsequent validity.

The following is the proper form to use if you wish to make any changes to your Will. Prepare it as you prepared your original Will, that is:

- Fill in the blanks in the form that follows;

- Type it on good quality paper;

- Assemble the 3 (three) witnesses and a Notary Public;

- Formally sign the Codicil as indicated in Chapter 8.

The following is a general form for a Codicil and standard clauses for changing provisions of your Will. Insert such changes as are necessary where indicated on the form and number each clause accordingly:

TITLE--MANDATORY

CODICIL TO THE LAST WILL AND TESTAMENT OF
[*your full name*] _____

IDENTIFICATION CLAUSE--MANDATORY

I, [*your full name as shown on your Will*] _____, a resident of [*city or town*] _____, [*county*] _____, [*state*] _____, make this Codicil to my Last Will and Testament dated [*date of your Will*] _____.

ADDITION TO YOUR WILL CLAUSE--OPTIONAL

☐ I add the following sentence to Clause [*number of clause*] _____ of my Will:

[*Here add whatever provision or change you desire.*]

REVOCATION OF PARAGRAPH OF WILL CLAUSE--OPTIONAL

☐   I revoke Clause [*number of clause*] _____ of my Will.

CORRECTION OF WILL CLAUSE--OPTIONAL

☐   I change Clause [*number of clause*] _____ of my Will to read as follows:

[*Here type the corrected paragraph.*]

SIGNATURE AND WITNESS CLAUSES--MANDATORY

I republish my Last Will and Testament dated [*date of Last Will and Testament*] _____ , as modified by this Codicil. I have signed this Codicil to my Will dated [*date of Last Will and Testament*] _____ , consisting of [*number of pages*] _____ typewritten pages, on [*month, date, and year*] _____ , and declare that I do so freely, for the purposes expressed, under no constraint or undue influence, and that I am of sound mind and of legal age.

[*signature of Testator*] _____
[*typewritten name of Testator*] _____

On [*month, date, and year*] _____, in the presence of all of us, the above-named testator published and signed this Codicil to [*his or her*] _____ Last Will and Testament, and then, at testator's request, and in testator's presence, and in each other's presence, we all signed below as witnesses, and we declare, under penalty of perjury, that, to the best of our knowledge, the testator signed this instrument freely, under no constraint or undue influence, and is of sound mind and legal age.

92

[*signature of Witness*] _____
[*typewritten name of Witness*] _____
[*address of Witness*] _____

[*signature of Witness*] _____
[*typewritten name of Witness*] _____
[*address of Witness*] _____

[*signature of Witness*] _____
[*typewritten name of Witness*] _____
[*address of Witness*] _____

SELF-PROVING AFFIDAVIT--MANDATORY

SELF-PROVING AFFIDAVIT

We, the undersigned testator and witnesses, being first sworn on oath, state that, in the presence of all the witnesses, the testator published and signed the above Codicil to [*his or her*] _____ Last Will and Testament and that, in the presence of the testator and of each other and at testator's request, each of the witnesses signed as witnesses, and that, to the best of our knowledge, the testator signed said Codicil freely, under no constraint or undue influence, and is of sound mind and legal age.

[*signature of Testator*] _____
[*typewritten name of Testator*] _____

[*signature of Witness*] _____
[*typewritten name of Witness*] _____
[*address of Witness*] _____

[*signature of Witness*] _____
[*typewritten name of Witness*]_____
[*address of Witness*] _____

[*signature of Witness*] _____
[*typewritten name of Witness*]_____
[*address of Witness*] _____

County of   } SS.
State of   }

Subscribed, sworn to and acknowledged before me on [*month, date, and year*] _____ by [*full name of testator*] _____, the testator, and by [*full name of first witness*] _____, [*full name of second witness*] _____, [*full name of third witness*] _____, the witnesses.

[*signature of Notary Public*] _____
[*typewritten name of Notary Public*] _____

Notary Public, in and for the
County of _____,
State of _____.

CHAPTER 10

A "LIVING" WILL

In this chapter, you will be given instructions on how to prepare a "Living" Will. A "Living" Will is a relatively new idea which has been made necessary by the advent of recent technological advances in the field of medicine which can allow for the continued existence of a person on advanced "life support" systems long after any normal semblance of "life", as many people consider it, has ceased.

The inherent problem which is raised by this type of extraordinary medical "life support" is that the person whose life is being artificially continued by such means may not wish to be kept alive beyond what they may consider to be the proper time for their life to end. However, since a person in such condition has no method of communicating their wishes to the medical and/or legal authorities in charge, a "Living" Will was developed which allows one to make these important decisions in advance of the situation.

As more and more advances are made in the medical field in terms of the ability to prevent "clinical" death, the difficult situations envisioned by a "Living" Will will occur more often. The legal acceptance of a "Living" Will is currently at the forefront of new laws being added in many states.

Although this "Living" Will does not address all possible contingencies regarding terminally ill patients, it does provide a written declaration for the individual to make known his or her decisions on life-prolonging procedures. This "Living" Will may be revoked, in most jurisdictions, by (1) a written revocation, (2) a destruction of the document or (3) an oral expression of your intent to revoke it.

If you desire that your life not be prolonged artificially when there is no reasonable chance for recovery and death is imminent, please follow the instructions below for completion of your "Living Will":

MANDATORY: the entire following form is mandatory. Please fill in the correct information in the appropriate blanks. You should have three witnesses sign the form. None of the witnesses should be a spouse or a blood relative. However, if possible, they should be persons who know you personally.

"LIVING" WILL OF *[your full name]* _____.

I, *[your full name]* _____, willfully and voluntarily make known my desire that my dying not be artificially prolonged under the circumstances set forth below, and I declare:

If at any time I should have a terminal condition and my attending physician has determined that there can be no recovery from such condition and my death is imminent, where the application of life prolonging procedures would serve only to artificially prolong the dying process, I direct that such procedures be withheld or withdrawn, and that I be permitted to die naturally with only the administration of medication or the performance of any medical procedure deemed necessary to provide me with comfort, care, or to alleviate pain.

In the absence of my ability to give directions regarding the use of such life prolonging procedures, it is my intention that this declaration shall be honored by my family and physician as the final expression of my legal right to refuse medical and surgical treatment and accept the consequences for such refusal.

I understand the full import of this declaration, and I am emotionally and mentally competent to make this declaration and Living Will.

This Living Will and Declaration made on [month, date, and year] _____.

[*signature of Signer*] _____
[*typewritten name of Signer*] _____

The above-signed person is personally known to me and I believe [*him or her*] _____ to be of sound mind.

[*signature of Witness*] _____
[*typewritten name of Witness*]_____
[*address of Witness*] _____

[*signature of Witness*] _____
[*typewritten name of Witness*]_____
[*address of Witness*] _____

[*signature of Witness*] _____
[*typewritten name of Witness*]_____
[*address of Witness*] _____

APPENDIX

STATE LAWS RELATING TO WILLS

The following listing contains a compilation of state laws relating to Wills for all fifty states and the District of Columbia. It is recommended that you review the listing which pertains to your home state and any state in which you own real estate before you complete your Will. The Will clauses used in this book are generally designed to overcome and eliminate most potential legal problems raised by any of these individual state laws. There may, however, be some information which will directly affect the manner in which you decide to prepare your Will.

As you review your state's particular laws, keep in mind that your Will will be interpreted under the laws of the state in which you reside at the time of your death. Your personal property will be distributed according to the laws of the state in which you were a resident at the time of your death. Your real estate, however, will be distributed under the laws of the state in which it is located, regardless of where you are a resident.

Every effort has been made to insure that this list is as complete and up-to-date as possible. However, state laws are subject to change. While most laws relating to Wills are relatively stable, it is advisable to check your particular state statutes to be certain there have been no major modifications since this book was prepared. To simplify this process as much as possible, the Statute book description of each state's laws have been included in the following list. By using this description, you may easily locate the appropriate laws at your local library. If you have any difficulty, your local librarian will be glad to help. Be forewarned, however, that most legislators are lawyers and that, therefore, much of your state's statutes will be written in a difficult-to-understand legal jargon. Use the Glossary located at the end of this book to translate this language.

The state-by-state listings in this Appendix contain the following information for each state:

- Relevant Statute or Law description.

- Minimum age requirements for disposing of real and personal property by Will.

- Required minimum number of witnesses (Be advised, however, that you should always use at least 3 (three) witnesses for your Will).

- Whether Witnesses may be beneficiaries under the Will. (Again, be advised that, to be safe, your witnesses should not be beneficiaries).

- The effect of divorce on the Will. (It is recommended that you review and change your Will if you are divorced).

- The effect of marriage on the Will. (It is recommended that you review and change your Will if you are married).

- Whether there are provisions for self-proving Wills. (To be prudent, you are advised to use the "self-proving affidavit" provided at the end of the Will clauses in Chapter 5).

- What parties must be mentioned in the Will. (Certain parties must be mentioned in your Will or they may be entitled to an intestate share of your estate regardless of your Will. Most states provide this protection for children born after a Will is made and for new spouses from a marriage after a Will is prepared. However, it is recommended that you review and change your Will if you adopt or have any new children, are married, or if any of your beneficiaries die).

- Spouse's right of election under the Will. (The surviving spouse's right to a certain share of the deceased spouse's estate regardless of any provisions in the Will of the deceased spouse).

- Whether the state follows the "Community Property" or "Common Law" system of ownership of marital property.

- Whether the state has restrictions on gifts to charities.

ALABAMA

State Statute or Law description: Alabama Code.

Minimum Age for disposing of property by Will: 18.

Required number of witnesses: Two. (Three are recommended).

May witnesses be beneficiaries?: Yes. (Not recommended).

Are there provisions for Self-Proving Wills?: Yes. (Use the Affidavit form in Chapter 5).

How does Divorce effect the Will?: Revokes the Will as to the divorced spouse.

How does Marriage effect the Will?: Revokes the Will as to the spouse if he/she is not otherwise provided for. Spouse may still be entitled to his/her statutory share under the state intestate laws.

Who must be mentioned in the Will ? Children, born or adopted; Surviving spouse.

Spouse's right to property regardless of Will: The surviving spouse is entitled to one-third of the "augmented" estate of the deceased spouse. In general, the "augmented" estate includes both the property that passes under the Will and any other property that passes by other "non-will" transfers, such as under the terms of a living trust or a joint tenancy arrangement.

Community Property or Common Law state?: Common Law.

State restrictions on gifts to charities?: No.

ALASKA

State Statute or Law description: Alaska Statutes.

Minimum Age for disposing of property by Will: 18.

Required number of witnesses: Two. (Three recommended).

May witnesses be beneficiaries?: Yes. (Not recommended).

Are there provisions for Self-Proving Wills?: Yes. (Use the Affidavit form in Chapter 5).

How does Divorce effect the Will?: Revokes the Will as to the divorced spouse.

How does Marriage effect the Will?: Revokes the Will as to the spouse if he/she is not otherwise provided for. Spouse may still be entitled to his/her statutory share under the state intestate laws.

Who must be mentioned in the Will ? Children, born or adopted; Surviving spouse.

Spouse's right to property regardless of Will: The surviving spouse is entitled to one-third of the "augmented" estate of the deceased spouse. In general, the "augmented" estate includes both the property that passes under the Will and any other property that passes by other "non-will" transfers, such as under the terms of a living trust or a joint tenancy arrangement.

Community Property or Common Law state?: Common Law.

State restrictions on gifts to charities?: No.

ARIZONA

State Statute or Law description: Arizona Revised Statutes Annotated.

Minimum Age for disposing of property by Will: 18.

Required number of witnesses: Two. (Three recommended).

May witnesses be beneficiaries?: Yes. (Not recommended).

Are there provisions for Self-Proving Wills?: Yes. (Use the Affidavit form in Chapter 5).

How does Divorce effect the Will?: Revokes the Will as to the divorced spouse.

How does Marriage effect the Will?: Revokes the Will as to the spouse if he/she is not otherwise provided for. Spouse may still be entitled to his/her statutory share under the state intestate laws.

Who must be mentioned in the Will ?: Children, born or adopted; Surviving spouse.

Spouse's right to property regardless of Will: Community property right to one-half of the deceased spouse's "community" property.

Community Property or Common Law state?: Community Property.

State restrictions on gifts to charities?: No.

ARKANSAS

State Statute or Law description: Arkansas Statutes Annotated.

Minimum Age for disposing of property by Will: 18.

Required number of witnesses: Two. (Three recommended).

May witnesses be beneficiaries?: No.

Are there provisions for Self-Proving Wills?: Yes. (Use the Affidavit form in Chapter 5).

How does Divorce effect the Will?: Revokes the Will as to the divorced spouse.

How does Marriage effect the Will?: Does not revoke the Will.

Who must be mentioned in the Will ?: Children, born or adopted; Surviving spouse.

Spouse's right to property regardless of Will: Intestate share, 1/3 of personal property and real estate for life

Community Property or Common Law state?: Common Law.

State restrictions on gifts to charities?: No.

CALIFORNIA

State Statute or Law description: California Probate Code.

Minimum Age for disposing of property by Will: 18.

Required number of witnesses: Two. (Three are recommended).

May witnesses be beneficiaries?: No.

Are there provisions for Self-Proving Wills?: No.

How does Divorce effect the Will?: Does not revoke the Will.

How does Marriage effect the Will?: Revokes the Will as to the surviving spouse.

Who must be mentioned in the Will ?: Children, born or adopted; Grandchildren of deceased child; Surviving spouse.

Spouse's right to property regardless of Will: Community property right to one-half of the deceased spouse's "community" property.

Community Property or Common Law state?: Community Property.

State restrictions on gifts to charities?: No.

COLORADO

State Statute or Law description: Colorado Revised Statutes Annotated.

Minimum Age for disposing of property by Will: 18.

Required number of witnesses: Two. (Three are recommended).

May witnesses be beneficiaries?: Yes. (Not recommended).

Are there provisions for Self-Proving Wills?: Yes. (Use the Affidavit form in Chapter 5).

How does Divorce effect the Will?: Revokes the Will as to the divorced spouse.

How does Marriage effect the Will?: Revokes the Will as to the spouse if he/she is not otherwise provided for. Spouse may still be entitled to his/her statutory share under the state intestate laws.

Who must be mentioned in the Will ?: Children, born or adopted; Surviving spouse.

Spouse's right to property regardless of Will: The surviving spouse is entitled to one-half of the "augmented" estate of the deceased spouse. In general, the "augmented" estate includes both the property that passes under the Will and any other property that passes by other "non-will" transfers, such as under the terms of a living trust or a joint tenancy arrangement.

Community Property or Common Law state?: Common Law.

State restrictions on gifts to charities?: No.

CONNECTICUT

State Statute or Law description: Connecticut General Statutes Annotated.

Minimum Age for disposing of property by Will: 18.

Required number of witnesses: Two. (Three are recommended).

May witnesses be beneficiaries?: No.

Are there provisions for Self-Proving Wills?: Yes. (Use the Affidavit form in Chapter 5).

How does Divorce effect the Will?: Revokes the Will completely.

How does Marriage effect the Will?: Revokes the Will completely.

Who must be mentioned in the Will ?: Children, born or adopted; Surviving spouse.

Spouse's right to property regardless of Will: The surviving spouse is entitled to one-third of the deceased spouse's real estate for the rest of his or her life.

Community Property or Common Law state?: Common Law.

State restrictions on gifts to charities?: No.

DELAWARE

State Statute or Law description: Delaware Code Annotated.

Minimum Age for disposing of property by Will: 18.

Required number of witnesses: Two. (Three are recommended).

May witnesses be beneficiaries?: Yes. (Not recommended).

Are there provisions for Self-Proving Wills?: Yes. (Use the Affidavit form in Chapter 5).

How does Divorce effect the Will?: Revokes the Will as to the divorced spouse.

How does Marriage effect the Will?: Does not revoke the Will.

Who must be mentioned in the Will ?: Children, born or adopted; Surviving spouse.

Spouse's right to property regardless of Will: The surviving spouse is entitled to one-third of the deceased spouse's estate or $20,000.00, whichever is less.

Community Property or Common Law state?: Common Law.

State restrictions on gifts to charities?: No.

FLORIDA

State Statute or Law description: Florida Statutes Annotated.

Minimum Age for disposing of property by Will: 18.

Required number of witnesses: Two. (Three are recommended).

May witnesses be beneficiaries?: Yes. (Not recommended).

Are there provisions for Self-Proving Wills?: Yes. (Use the Affidavit form in Chapter 5).

How does Divorce effect the Will?: Revokes the Will as to the divorced spouse.

How does Marriage effect the Will?: Revokes the Will as to the spouse if he/she is not otherwise provided for. Spouse may still be entitled to his/her statutory share under the state intestate laws.

Who must be mentioned in the Will ?: Children, born or adopted; Surviving spouse.

Spouse's right to property regardless of Will: The surviving spouse is entitled to 30% of the deceased spouse's estate.

Community Property or Common Law state?: Common Law.

State restrictions on gifts to charities?: Yes. If extensive gifts to charities are contemplated, please refer directly to statute or consult an attorney.

GEORGIA

State Statute or Law description: Georgia Code.

Minimum Age for disposing of property by Will: 14.

Required number of witnesses: Two. (Three are recommended).

May witnesses be beneficiaries?: No.

Are there provisions for Self-Proving Wills?: Yes. (Use the Affidavit form in Chapter 5).

How does Divorce effect the Will?: Revokes the Will completely.

How does Marriage effect the Will?: Revokes the Will completely.

Who must be mentioned in the Will ?: Statute contains detailed provisions regarding this matter. Please refer directly to statute text or consult an attorney if this is a critical factor.

Spouse's right to property regardless of Will: The surviving spouse is entitled to one year's support from the deceased spouse's estate.

Community Property or Common Law state?: Common Law.

State restrictions on gifts to charities?: Yes. If extensive gifts to charities are contemplated, please refer directly to statute or consult an attorney.

HAWAII

State Statute or Law description: Hawaii Revised Statutes.

Minimum Age for disposing of property by Will: 18.

Required number of witnesses: Two. (Three are recommended).

May witnesses be beneficiaries?: Yes. (Not recommended).

Are there provisions for Self-Proving Wills?: Yes. (Use the Affidavit form in Chapter 5).

How does Divorce effect the Will?: Revokes the Will as to the divorced spouse.

How does Marriage effect the Will?: Revokes the Will as to the spouse if he/she is not otherwise provided for. Spouse may still be entitled to his/her statutory share under the state intestate laws.

Who must be mentioned in the Will ?: Children, born or adopted; Surviving spouse.

Spouse's right to property regardless of Will: The surviving spouse is entitled to one-third of the deceased spouse's estate.

Community Property or Common Law state?: Common Law.

State restrictions on gifts to charities?: No.

IDAHO

State Statute or Law description: Idaho Code.

Minimum Age for disposing of property by Will: 18.

Required number of witnesses: Two. (Three are recommended).

May witnesses be beneficiaries?: Yes. (Not recommended).

Are there provisions for Self-Proving Wills?: Yes. (Use the Affidavit form in Chapter 5).

How does Divorce effect the Will?: Revokes the Will as to the divorced spouse.

How does Marriage effect the Will?: Revokes the Will as to the spouse if he/she is not otherwise provided for. Spouse may still be entitled to his/her statutory share under the state intestate laws.

Who must be mentioned in the Will ?: Children, born or adopted; Surviving spouse.

Spouse's right to property regardless of Will: Community property right to one-half of the deceased spouse's "community" property.

Community Property or Common Law state?: Community Property.

State restrictions on gifts to charities?: Yes. If extensive gifts to charities are contemplated, please refer directly to statute or consult an attorney.

ILLINOIS

State Statute or Law description: Illinois Annotated Statutes.

Minimum Age for disposing of property by Will: 18.

Required number of witnesses: Two. (Three are recommended).

May witnesses be beneficiaries?: No.

Are there provisions for Self-Proving Wills?: Yes. (Use the Affidavit form in Chapter 5).

How does Divorce effect the Will?: Revokes the Will as to the divorced spouse.

How does Marriage effect the Will?: Does not revoke the Will.

Who must be mentioned in the Will ?: Children, born or adopted; Surviving spouse.

Spouse's right to property regardless of Will: Generally, the surviving spouse is entitled to one-half of the deceased spouse's estate if there are no children, and only one-third if there are children. However, please refer directly to the statute as the provisions are detailed.

Community Property or Common law state?: Common Law.

State restrictions on gifts to charities?: No.

INDIANA

State Statute or Law description: Indiana Code Annotated.

Minimum Age for disposing of property by Will: 18, or member of Armed Forces or Merchant Marine.

Required number of witnesses: Two. (Three are recommended).

May witnesses be beneficiaries?: No.

Are there provisions for Self-Proving Wills?: Yes. (Use the Affidavit form in Chapter 5).

How does Divorce effect the Will?: Revokes the Will as to the divorced spouse.

How does Marriage effect the Will?: Does not revoke the Will.

Who must be mentioned in the Will ?: Children, born or adopted; Surviving spouse.

Spouse's right to property regardless of Will: The surviving spouse is entitled to one-third of the deceased spouse's estate.

Community Property or Common Law state?: Common Law.

State restrictions on gifts to charities?: No.

IOWA

State Statute or Law description: Iowa Code Annotated.

Minimum Age for disposing of property by Will: 18.

Required number of witnesses: Two. (Three are recommended).

May witnesses be beneficiaries?: No.

Are there provisions for Self-Proving Wills?: Yes. (Use the Affidavit form in Chapter 5).

How does Divorce effect the Will?: Generally does not revoke the Will.

How does Marriage effect the Will?: Revokes the Will as to the spouse if he/she is not otherwise provided for. Spouse may still be entitled to his/her statutory share under the state intestate laws.

Who must be mentioned in the Will ?: Children, born or adopted; Surviving spouse.

Spouse's right to property regardless of Will: The surviving spouse is entitled to one-third of the deceased spouse's estate.

Community Property or Common Law state?: Common Law.

State restrictions on gifts to charities?: No.

KANSAS

State Statute or Law description: Kansas Statutes Annotated.

Minimum Age for disposing of property by Will: 18.

Required number of witnesses: Two. (Three are recommended).

May witnesses be beneficiaries?: Yes. (Not recommended).

Are there provisions for Self-Proving Wills?: Yes. (Use the Affidavit form in Chapter 5).

How does Divorce effect the Will?: Revokes the Will as to the divorced spouse.

How does Marriage effect the Will?: Revokes the Will if a child is later born to or adopted into the marriage.

Who must be mentioned in the Will ?: Surviving spouse.

Spouse's right to property regardless of Will: Generally, the surviving spouse is entitled to one-half of the deceased spouse's estate if there are no children, and only one-third if there are children. However, please refer directly to the statute as the provisions are detailed.

Community Property or Common law state?: Common Law.

State restrictions on gifts to charities?: No.

KENTUCKY

State Statute or Law description: Kentucky Revised Statutes.

Minimum Age for disposing of property by Will: 18.

Required number of witnesses: Two. (Three are recommended).

May witnesses be beneficiaries?: No.

Are there provisions for Self-Proving Wills?: Yes. (Use the Affidavit form in Chapter 5).

How does Divorce effect the Will?: Revokes the Will as to the divorced spouse.

How does Marriage effect the Will?: Revokes the Will completely.

Who must be mentioned in the Will ?: Children, born or adopted; Surviving spouse.

Spouse's right to property regardless of Will: The surviving spouse is entitled to one-third of the deceased spouse's real estate for the rest of his or her life.

Community Property or Common Law state?: Common Law.

State restrictions on gifts to charities?: No.

LOUISIANA

State Statute or Law description: Louisiana Revised Statutes.

Minimum Age for disposing of property by Will: 16.

Required number of witnesses: Three.

May witnesses be beneficiaries?: No.

Are there provisions for Self-Proving Wills?: Yes. (Use the Affidavit form in Chapter 5).

How does Divorce effect the Will?: Does not revoke the Will.

How does Marriage effect the Will?: Does not revoke the Will.

Who must be mentioned in the Will ?: Children, born or adopted; Surviving spouse.

Spouse's right to property regardless of Will: The Louisiana Civil Code provisions regarding this matter are detailed and should be consulted directly.   (NOTE: Children   are   also   protected   from   total disinheritance in Louisiana).

Community Property or Common Law state?: Louisiana Civil Code (The laws of Louisiana are unique to the United States in that they are patterned after the French Civil Code. Please refer to the code directly if you have any questions or consult an attorney).

State restrictions on gifts to charities?: No.

MAINE

State Statute or Law description: Maine Revised Statutes Annotated.

Minimum Age for disposing of property by Will: 18, married, or a surviving spouse.

Required number of witnesses: Three.

May witnesses be beneficiaries?: Yes. (Not recommended).

Are there provisions for Self-Proving Wills?: Yes. (Use the Affidavit form in Chapter 5).

How does Divorce effect the Will?: Revokes the Will as to the divorced spouse.

How does Marriage effect the Will?: Revokes the Will as to the spouse if he/she is not otherwise provided for. Spouse may still be entitled to his/her statutory share under the state intestate laws.

Who must be mentioned in the Will ?: Children, born or adopted; Grandchildren of deceased child; Surviving spouse.

Spouse's right to property regardless of Will: The surviving spouse is entitled to one-third of the "augmented" estate of the deceased spouse. In general, the "augmented" estate includes both the property that passes under the Will and any other property that passes by other "non-will" transfers, such as under the terms of a living trust or a joint tenancy arrangement.

Community Property or Common Law state?: Common Law.

State restrictions on gifts to charities?: No.

MARYLAND

State Statute or Law description: Maryland Code Annotated.

Minimum Age for disposing of property by Will: 18.

Required number of witnesses: Two. (Three are recommended).

May witnesses be beneficiaries?: Yes. (Not recommended).

Are there provisions for Self-Proving Wills?: No.

How does Divorce effect the Will?: Revokes the Will as to the divorced spouse.

How does Marriage effect the Will?: Revokes the Will if a child is later born to or adopted into the marriage and survives the maker of the Will

Who must be mentioned in the Will ?: Children, born or adopted; Grandchildren (of deceased child); Surviving spouse.

Spouse's right to property regardless of Will: Generally, the surviving spouse is entitled to one-half of the deceased spouse's estate if there are no children, and only one-third if there are children. However, please refer directly to the statute as the provisions are detailed.

Community Property or Common law state?: Common Law.

State restrictions on gifts to charities?: No.

MASSACHUSETTS

State Statute or Law description: Massachusetts General Laws Annotated.

Minimum Age for disposing of property by Will: 18.

Required number of witnesses: Two. (Three are recommended).

May witnesses be beneficiaries?: No.

Are there provisions for Self-Proving Wills?: Yes. (Use the Affidavit form in Chapter 5).

How does Divorce effect the Will?: Revokes the Will as to the divorced spouse.

How does Marriage effect the Will?: Revokes the Will.

Who must be mentioned in the Will ?: Children, born or adopted; Grandchildren (if of deceased child); Surviving spouse.

Spouse's right to property regardless of Will: Generally, the surviving spouse is entitled to one-half of the deceased spouse's estate if there are no children, and only one-third if there are children. However, please refer directly to the statute as the provisions are detailed.

Community Property or Common law state?: Common Law.

State restrictions on gifts to charities?: No.

MICHIGAN

State Statute or Law description: Michigan Compiled Laws Annotated.

Minimum Age for disposing of property by Will: 18.

Required number of witnesses: Two. (Three are recommended).

May witnesses be beneficiaries?: No.

Are there provisions for Self-Proving Wills?: No.

How does Divorce effect the Will?: Revokes the Will as to the divorced spouse.

How does Marriage effect the Will?: Revokes the Will as to the spouse if he/she is not otherwise provided for. Spouse may still be entitled to his/her statutory share under the state intestate laws.

Who must be mentioned in the Will ?: Children, born or adopted; Surviving spouse.

Spouse's right to property regardless of Will: Generally, the surviving spouse is entitled to one-half of the deceased spouse's estate if there are no children, and only one-third if there are children. However, please refer directly to the statute as the provisions are detailed.

Community Property or Common Law state?: Common Law.

State restrictions on gifts to charities?: No.

MINNESOTA

State Statute or Law description: Minnesota Statutes Annotated.

Minimum Age for disposing of property by Will: 18.

Required number of witnesses: Two. (Three are recommended).

May witnesses be beneficiaries?: Yes. (Not recommended).

Are there provisions for Self-Proving Wills?: Yes. (Use the Affidavit form in Chapter 5).

How does Divorce effect the Will?: Revokes the Will as to the divorced spouse.

How does Marriage effect the Will?: Revokes the Will as to the spouse if he/she is not otherwise provided for. Spouse may still be entitled to his/her statutory share under the state intestate laws.

Who must be mentioned in the Will ?: Children, born or adopted; Grandchildren (if of deceased child); Surviving spouse.

Spouse's right to property regardless of Will: Generally, the surviving spouse is entitled to one-half of the deceased spouse's estate if there are no children, and only one-third if there are children. However, please refer directly to the statute as the provisions are detailed.

Community Property or Common Law state?: Common Law.

State restrictions on gifts to charities?: No.

MISSISSIPPI

State Statute or Law description: Mississippi Code Annotated.

Minimum Age for disposing of property by Will: 18.

Required number of witnesses: Two. (Three are recommended).

May witnesses be beneficiaries?: No.

Are there provisions for Self-Proving Wills?: Yes. (Use the Affidavit form in Chapter 5).

How does Divorce effect the Will?: Does not revoke the Will.

How does Marriage effect the Will?: Does not revoke the Will.

Who must be mentioned in the Will?: Children, born or adopted; Surviving spouse.

Spouse's right to property regardless of Will: Generally, the surviving spouse is entitled to one-half of the deceased spouse's estate if there are no children, and only one-third if there are children. However, please refer directly to the statute as the provisions are detailed.

Community Property or Common Law state?: Common Law.

State restrictions on gifts to charities?: Yes. If extensive gifts to charities are contemplated, please refer directly to statute or consult an attorney.

MISSOURI

State Statute or Law description: Missouri Annotated Statutes.

Minimum Age for disposing of property by Will: 18.

Required number of witnesses: Two. (Three are recommended).

May witnesses be beneficiaries?: No.

Are there provisions for Self-Proving Wills?: Yes. (Use the Affidavit form in Chapter 5).

How does Divorce effect the Will?: Revokes the Will as to the divorced spouse.

How does Marriage effect the Will?: Revokes the Will as to the spouse if he/she is not otherwise provided for. Spouse may still be entitled to his/her statutory share under the state intestate laws.

Who must be mentioned in the Will ?: Children, born or adopted; Surviving spouse.

Spouse's right to property regardless of Will: Generally, the surviving spouse is entitled to one-half of the deceased spouse's estate if there are no children, and only one-third if there are children. However, please refer directly to the statute as the provisions are detailed.

Community Property or Common Law state?: Common Law.

State restrictions on gifts to charities?: No.

MONTANA

State Statute or Law description: Montana Code Annotated.

Minimum Age for disposing of property by Will: 18.

Required number of witnesses: Two. (Three are recommended).

May witnesses be beneficiaries?: No.

Are there provisions for Self-Proving Wills?: Yes. (Use the Affidavit form in Chapter 5).

How does Divorce effect the Will?: Revokes the Will as to the divorced spouse.

How does Marriage effect the Will?: Revokes the Will as to the spouse if he/she is not otherwise provided for. Spouse may still be entitled to his/her statutory share under the state intestate laws.

Who must be mentioned in the Will ?: Children, born or adopted; Surviving spouse.

Spouse's right to property regardless of Will: The surviving spouse is entitled to one-third of the "augmented" estate of the deceased spouse. In general, the "augmented" estate includes both the property that passes under the Will and any other property that passes by other "non-will" transfers, such as under the terms of a living trust or a joint tenancy arrangement.

Community Property or Common Law state?: Common Law.

State restrictions on gifts to charities?: Yes. If extensive gifts to charities are contemplated, please refer directly to statute or consult an attorney.

NEBRASKA

State Statute or Law description: Nebraska Revised Statutes.

Minimum Age for disposing of property by Will: 18.

Required number of witnesses: Two. (Three are recommended).

May witnesses be beneficiaries?: Yes. (Not recommended).

Are there provisions for Self-Proving Wills?: Yes. (Use the Affidavit form in Chapter 5).

How does Divorce effect the Will?: Revokes the Will as to the divorced spouse.

How does Marriage effect the Will?: Revokes the Will as to the spouse if he/she is not otherwise provided for. Spouse may still be entitled to his/her statutory share under the state intestate laws.

Who must be mentioned in the Will ?: Children, born or adopted; Surviving spouse.

Spouse's right to property regardless of Will: The surviving spouse is entitled to one-third of the "augmented" estate of the deceased spouse. In general, the "augmented" estate includes both the property that passes under the Will and any other property that passes by other "non-will" transfers, such as under the terms of a living trust or a joint tenancy arrangement.

Community Property or Common Law state?: Common Law.

State restrictions on gifts to charities?: No.

NEVADA

State Statute or Law description: Nevada Revised Statutes Annotated.

Minimum Age for disposing of property by Will: 18.

Required number of witnesses: Two. (Three are recommended).

May witnesses be beneficiaries?: No.

Are there provisions for Self-Proving Wills?: Yes. (Use the Affidavit form in Chapter 5).

How does Divorce effect the Will?: Revokes the Will as to the divorced spouse.

How does Marriage effect the Will?: Revokes the Will as to the spouse if he/she is not otherwise provided for. Spouse may still be entitled to his/her statutory share under the state intestate laws.

Who must be mentioned in the Will ?: Statute contains detailed provisions regarding this matter. Please refer directly to statute text or consult an attorney if this is a critical factor.

Spouse's right to property regardless of Will: Community property right to one-half of the deceased spouse's "community" property.

Community Property or Common Law state?: Community Property.

State restrictions on gifts to charities?: No.

NEW HAMPSHIRE

State Statute or Law description: New Hampshire Revised Statutes Annotated.

Minimum Age for disposing of property by Will: 18, or married.

Required number of witnesses: Three.

May witnesses be beneficiaries?: No.

Are there provisions for Self-Proving Wills?: Yes. (If you wish to use a Self-proving Affidavit, please consult an attorney).

How does Divorce effect the Will?: Does not revoke the Will.

How does Marriage effect the Will?: Revokes the Will if a child is later born to the marriage.

Who must be mentioned in the Will ?: Children, born or adopted; Grandchildren; Surviving spouse.

Spouse's right to property regardless of Will: Generally, the surviving spouse is entitled to one-half of the deceased spouse's estate if there are no children, and only one-third if there are children. However, please refer directly to the statute as the provisions are detailed.

Community Property or Common Law state?: Common Law.

State restrictions on gifts to charities?: No.

NEW JERSEY

State Statute or Law description: New Jersey Revised Statutes Annotated.

Minimum Age for disposing of property by Will: 21.

Required number of witnesses: Two. (Three are recommended).

May witnesses be beneficiaries?: Yes. (Not recommended).

Are there provisions for Self-Proving Wills?: Yes. (Use the Affidavit form
in Chapter 5).

How does Divorce effect the Will?: Revokes the Will as to the divorced
spouse.

How does Marriage effect the Will?: Revokes the Will as to the spouse if
he/she is not otherwise provided for. Spouse may still be entitled to
his/her statutory share under the state intestate laws.

Who must be mentioned in the Will ?: Children, born or adopted;
Grandchildren; Surviving spouse.

Spouse's right to property regardless of Will: The surviving spouse is
entitled to one-third of the "augmented" estate of the deceased
spouse. In general, the "augmented" estate includes both the
property that passes under the Will and any other property that
passes by other "non-will" transfers, such as under the terms of a
living trust or a joint tenancy arrangement.

Community Property or Common Law state?: Common Law.

State restrictions on gifts to charities?: No.

NEW MEXICO

State Statute or Law description: New Mexico Statutes Annotated.

Minimum Age for disposing of property by Will: 18.

Required number of witnesses: Two. (Three are recommended).

May witnesses be beneficiaries?: Yes. (Not recommended).

Are there provisions for Self-Proving Wills?: Yes. (Use the Affidavit form in Chapter 5).

How does Divorce effect the Will?: Revokes the Will as to the divorced spouse.

How does Marriage effect the Will?: Revokes the Will as to the spouse if he/she is not otherwise provided for. Spouse may still be entitled to his/her statutory share under the state intestate laws.

Who must be mentioned in the Will ?: Children, born or adopted; Surviving spouse.

Spouse's right to property regardless of Will: Community property right to one-half of the deceased spouse's "community" property.

Community Property or Common Law state?: Community Property.

State restrictions on gifts to charities?: No.

NEW YORK

State Statute or Law description: New York Law.

Minimum Age for disposing of property by Will: 18.

Required number of witnesses: Two. (Three are recommended).

May witnesses be beneficiaries?: No.

Are there provisions for Self-Proving Wills?: Yes. (Use the Affidavit form in Chapter 5).

How does Divorce effect the Will?: Revokes the Will as to the divorced spouse.

How does Marriage effect the Will?: Does not revoke the Will.

Who must be mentioned in the Will ?: Children, born or adopted; Surviving spouse.

Spouse's right to property regardless of Will: Generally, the surviving spouse is entitled to one-half of the deceased spouse's estate if there are no children, and only one-third if there are children. However, please refer directly to the statute as the provisions are detailed.

Community Property or Common Law state?: Common Law.

State restrictions on gifts to charities?: No.

NORTH CAROLINA

State Statute or Law description: North Carolina General Statutes.

Minimum Age for disposing of property by Will: 18.

Required number of witnesses: Two. (Three are recommended).

May witnesses be beneficiaries?: No.

Are there provisions for Self-Proving Wills?: Yes. (Use the Affidavit form in Chapter 5).

How does Divorce effect the Will?: Revokes the Will as to the divorced spouse.

How does Marriage effect the Will?: Does not revoke the Will.

Who must be mentioned in the Will ?: Children, born or adopted; Surviving spouse.

Spouse's right to property regardless of Will: Generally, the surviving spouse is entitled to one-half of the deceased spouse's estate if there are no children, and only one-third if there are children. However, please refer directly to the statute as the provisions are detailed.

Community Property or Common Law state?: Common Law.

State restrictions on gifts to charities?: No.

NORTH DAKOTA

State Statute or Law description: North Dakota Century Code.

Minimum Age for disposing of property by Will: 18.

Required number of witnesses: Two. (Three are recommended).

May witnesses be beneficiaries?: Yes. (Not recommended).

Are there provisions for Self-Proving Wills?: Yes. (Use the Affidavit form in Chapter 5).

How does Divorce effect the Will?: Revokes the Will as to the divorced spouse.

How does Marriage effect the Will?: Revokes the Will as to the spouse if he/she is not otherwise provided for. Spouse may still be entitled to his/her statutory share under the state intestate laws.

Who must be mentioned in the Will ?: Children, born or adopted; Surviving spouse.

Spouse's right to property regardless of Will: The surviving spouse is entitled to one-third of the "augmented" estate of the deceased spouse. In general, the "augmented" estate includes both the property that passes under the Will and any other property that passes by other "non-will" transfers, such as under the terms of a living trust or a joint tenancy arrangement.

Community Property or Common Law state?: Common Law.

State restrictions on gifts to charities?: No.

OHIO

State Statute or Law description: Ohio Revised Code Annotated.

Minimum Age for disposing of property by Will: 18.

Required number of witnesses: Two. (Three are recommended).

May witnesses be beneficiaries?: No.

Are there provisions for Self-Proving Wills?: No.

How does Divorce effect the Will?: Revokes the Will as to the divorced spouse.

How does Marriage effect the Will?: Does not revoke the Will.

Who must be mentioned in the Will ?: Children, born or adopted; Surviving spouse.

Spouse's right to property regardless of Will: Generally, the surviving spouse is entitled to one-half of the deceased spouse's estate if there are no children, and only one-third if there are children. However, please refer directly to the statute as the provisions are detailed.

Community Property or Common Law state?: Common Law.

State restrictions on gifts to charities?: Yes. If extensive gifts to charities are contemplated, please refer directly to statute or consult an attorney.

OKLAHOMA

State Statute or Law description: Oklahoma Statutes Annotated.

Minimum Age for disposing of property by Will: 18.

Required number of witnesses: Two. (Three are recommended).

May witnesses be beneficiaries?: Yes. (Not recommended).

Are there provisions for Self-Proving Wills?: Yes. (Use the Affidavit form
    in Chapter 5).

How does Divorce effect the Will?: Revokes the Will as to the divorced
    spouse.

How does Marriage effect the Will?: Revokes the Will if a child is later born
    into the marriage.

Who must be mentioned in the Will ?: Children, born or adopted; Surviving
    spouse.

Spouse's right to property regardless of Will: Generally, the surviving
    spouse is entitled to one-half of the deceased spouse's estate if there
    are no children, and only one-third if there are children. However,
    please refer directly to the statute as the provisions are detailed.

Community Property or Common Law state?: Common Law.

State restrictions on gifts to charities?: No.

OREGON

State Statute or Law description: Oregon Revised Statutes.

Minimum Age for disposing of property by Will: 18.

Required number of witnesses: Two. (Three are recommended).

May witnesses be beneficiaries?: Yes. (Not recommended).

Are there provisions for Self-Proving Wills?: Yes. (Use the Affidavit form in Chapter 5).

How does Divorce effect the Will?: Revokes the Will as to the divorced spouse.

How does Marriage effect the Will?: Revokes the Will if the maker of the Will is survived by a spouse.

Who must be mentioned in the Will ?: Statute contains detailed provisions regarding this matter. Please refer directly to statute text or consult an attorney if this is a critical factor.Spouse's right to property regardless of Will:

Spouse's right to property regardless of Will: The surviving spouse is entitled to one-fourth of the deceased spouse's estate.

Community Property or Common Law state?: Common Law.

State restrictions on gifts to charities?: No.

PENNSYLVANIA

State Statute or Law description: Pennsylvania Cons. Statutes Annotated.

Minimum Age for disposing of property by Will: 18.

Required number of witnesses: Three.

May witnesses be beneficiaries?: Yes. (Not recommended).

Are there provisions for Self-Proving Wills?: Yes. (Use the Affidavit form in Chapter 5).

How does Divorce effect the Will?: Revokes the Will as to the divorced spouse.

How does Marriage effect the Will?: Revokes the Will as to the spouse if he/she is not otherwise provided for. Spouse may still be entitled to his/her statutory share under the state intestate laws.

Who must be mentioned in the Will ?: Children, born or adopted; Surviving spouse.

Spouse's right to property regardless of Will: The surviving spouse is entitled to one-third of the deceased spouse's estate.

Community Property or Common Law state?: Common Law.

State restrictions on gifts to charities?: No.

RHODE ISLAND

State Statute or Law description: Rhode Island General Laws.

Minimum Age for disposing of property by Will: 18.

Required number of witnesses: Two. (Three are recommended).

May witnesses be beneficiaries?: No.

Are there provisions for Self-Proving Wills?: Yes. (Use the Affidavit form in Chapter 5).

How does Divorce effect the Will?: Does not revoke the Will.

How does Marriage effect the Will?: Revokes the Will completely.

Who must be mentioned in the Will ?: Children, born or adopted; Grandchildren (if of deceased child); Surviving spouse.

Spouse's right to property regardless of Will: The surviving spouse is entitled to one-third of the deceased spouse's real estate for the rest of his or her life.

Community Property or Common Law state?: Common Law.

State restrictions on gifts to charities?: No.

SOUTH CAROLINA

State Statute or Law description: South Carolina Code Annotated.

Minimum Age for disposing of property by Will: 18.

Required number of witnesses: Three.

May witnesses be beneficiaries?: Generally, Yes. (Not recommended).

Are there provisions for Self-Proving Wills?: Yes. (Use the Affidavit form in Chapter 5).

How does Divorce effect the Will?: Revokes the Will as to the divorced spouse.

How does Marriage effect the Will?: Revokes the Will if spouse, children or grandchildren survive the maker of the Will.

Who must be mentioned in the Will ?: Children, born or adopted; Surviving spouse.

Spouse's right to property regardless of Will: The surviving spouse is entitled to one-third of the deceased spouse's real estate for the rest of his or her life.

Community Property or Common Law state?: Common Law.

State restrictions on gifts to charities?: No.

SOUTH DAKOTA

State Statute or Law description: South Dakota Codified Laws Annotated.

Minimum Age for disposing of property by Will: 18.

Required number of witnesses: Two. (Three are recommended).

May witnesses be beneficiaries?: No.

Are there provisions for Self-Proving Wills?: Yes. (Use the Affidavit form in Chapter 5).

How does Divorce effect the Will?: Does not revoke the Will.

How does Marriage effect the Will?: Revokes the Will if spouse, child or grandchildren survive the maker of the Will.

Who must be mentioned in the Will ?: Statute contains detailed provisions regarding this matter. Please refer directly to statute text or consult an attorney if this is a critical factor.

Spouse's right to property regardless of Will: The surviving spouse is entitled to one-third of the "augmented" estate of the deceased spouse. In general, the "augmented" estate includes both the property that passes under the Will and any other property that passes by other "non-will" transfers, such as under the terms of a living trust or a joint tenancy arrangement.

Community Property or Common Law state?: Common Law.

State restrictions on gifts to charities?: No.

TENNESSEE

State Statute or Law description: Tennessee Code Annotated.

Minimum Age for disposing of property by Will: 18.

Required number of witnesses: Two. (Three are recommended).

May witnesses be beneficiaries?: No.

Are there provisions for Self-Proving Wills?: Yes. (Use the Affidavit form in Chapter 5).

How does Divorce effect the Will?: Revokes the Will as to the divorced spouse.

How does Marriage effect the Will?: Revokes the Will if a child is later born to the marriage.

Who must be mentioned in the Will?: Children, born or adopted; Surviving spouse.

Spouse's right to property regardless of Will: The surviving spouse is entitled to one-third of the deceased spouse's estate.

Community Property or Common Law state?: Common Law.

State restrictions on gifts to charities?: No.

TEXAS

State Statute or Law description: Texas Code Annotated.

Minimum Age for disposing of property by Will: 18, or married.

Required number of witnesses: Two. (Three are recommended).

May witnesses be beneficiaries?: Generally, yes. (Not recommended).

Are there provisions for Self-Proving Wills?: Yes. (Use the Affidavit form in Chapter 5).

How does Divorce effect the Will?: Revokes the Will as to the divorced spouse.

How does Marriage effect the Will?: Does not revoke the Will.

Who must be mentioned in the Will?: Children, born or adopted.

Spouse's right to property regardless of Will: Community property right to one-half of the deceased spouse's "community" property.

Community Property or Common Law state?: Community Property.

State restrictions on gifts to charities?: No.

UTAH

State Statute or Law description: Utah Code Annotated.

Minimum Age for disposing of property by Will: 18.

Required number of witnesses: Two. (Three are recommended).

May witnesses be beneficiaries?: Yes. (Not recommended).

Are there provisions for Self-Proving Wills?: Yes. (Use the Affidavit form in Chapter 5).

How does Divorce effect the Will?: Revokes the Will as to the divorced spouse.

How does Marriage effect the Will?: Revokes the Will as to the spouse if he/she is not otherwise provided for. Spouse may still be entitled to his/her statutory share under the state intestate laws.

Who must be mentioned in the Will?:   Children, born or adopted; Grandchildren (if of deceased child); Surviving spouse.

Spouse's right to property regardless of Will: The surviving spouse is entitled to one-third of the deceased spouse's estate.

Community Property or Common Law state?: Common Law.

State restrictions on gifts to charities?: No.

VERMONT

State Statute or Law description: Vermont Statutes Annotated.

Minimum Age for disposing of property by Will: 18.

Required number of witnesses: Three.

May witnesses be beneficiaries?: No.

Are there provisions for Self-Proving Wills?: No.

How does Divorce effect the Will?: Does not revoke the Will.

How does Marriage effect the Will?: Does not revoke the Will.

Who must be mentioned in the Will?: Children, born or adopted; Grandchildren (if of deceased child); Surviving spouse.

Spouse's right to property regardless of Will: The surviving spouse is entitled to one-third of the deceased spouse's real estate for the rest of his or her life.

Community Property or Common Law state?: Common Law.

State restrictions on gifts to charities?: No.

VIRGINIA

State Statute or Law description: Virginia Code Annotated.

Minimum Age for disposing of property by Will: 18.

Required number of witnesses: Two. (Three are recommended).

May witnesses be beneficiaries?: No.

Are there provisions for Self-Proving Wills?: Yes. (Use the Affidavit form in Chapter 5).

How does Divorce effect the Will?: Revokes the Will as to the divorced spouse.

How does Marriage effect the Will?: Does not revoke the Will.

Who must be mentioned in the Will?: Children, born or adopted; Grandchildren (if of deceased child); Surviving spouse.

Spouse's right to property regardless of Will: The surviving spouse is entitled to one-third of the deceased spouse's real estate for the rest of his or her life.

Community Property or Common Law state?: Common Law.

State restrictions on gifts to charities?: No.

WASHINGTON

State Statute or Law description: Washington Revised Code Annotated.

Minimum Age for disposing of property by Will: 18.

Required number of witnesses: Two. (Three are recommended).

May witnesses be beneficiaries?: No.

Are there provisions for Self-Proving Wills?: Yes. (Use the Affidavit form in Chapter 5).

How does Divorce effect the Will?: Revokes the Will as to the divorced spouse.

How does Marriage effect the Will?: Revokes the Will as to the surviving spouse.

Who must be mentioned in the Will?: Statute contains detailed provisions regarding this matter. Please refer directly to statute text or consult an attorney if this is a critical factor.

Spouse's right to property regardless of Will: Community property right to one-half of the deceased spouse's "community" property.

Community Property or Common Law state?: Community Property.

State restrictions on gifts to charities?: No.

WEST VIRGINIA

State Statute or Law description: West Virginia Code Annotated.

Minimum Age for disposing of property by Will: 18.

Required number of witnesses: Two. (Three are recommended).

May witnesses be beneficiaries?: No.

Are there provisions for Self-Proving Wills?: Yes. (Use the Affidavit form in Chapter 5).

How does Divorce effect the Will?: Revokes the Will completely.

How does Marriage effect the Will?: Revokes the Will completely.

Who must be mentioned in the Will?: Children, born or adopted; Grandchildren ; Surviving spouse.

Spouse's right to property regardless of Will: The surviving spouse is entitled to one-third of the deceased spouse's real estate for the rest of his or her life.

Community Property or Common Law state?: Common Law.

State restrictions on gifts to charities?: No.

WISCONSIN

State Statute or Law description: Wisconsin Statutes Annotated.

Minimum Age for disposing of property by Will: 18.

Required number of witnesses: Two. (Three are recommended).

May witnesses be beneficiaries?: No.

Are there provisions for Self-Proving Wills?: No.

How does Divorce effect the Will?: Revokes the Will as to the divorced spouse.

How does Marriage effect the Will?: Revokes the Will as to the spouse if he/she is not otherwise provided for. Spouse may still be entitled to his/her statutory share under the state intestate laws.

Who must be mentioned in the Will?: Children, born or adopted; Grandchildren (if of deceased child); Surviving spouse.

Spouse's right to property regardless of Will: Modified community property right to one-half of the deceased spouse's "community" property.

Community Property or Common Law state?: Common Law. (However, please note that Wisconsin has in place a marital property act which treats property held in a marriage in essentially the same manner that it is treated in "Community Property" states. The Wisconsin law, however, uses a unique terminology to describe this treatment of property.

State restrictions on gifts to charities?:   No.

WYOMING

State Statute or Law description: Wyoming Statutes.

Minimum Age for disposing of property by Will: 18.

Required number of witnesses: Two. (Three are recommended).

May witnesses be beneficiaries?: No.

Are there provisions for Self-Proving Wills?: Yes. (Use the Affidavit form in Chapter 5).

How does Divorce effect the Will?: Revokes the Will as to the divorced spouse.

How does Marriage effect the Will?: Does not revoke the Will.

Who must be mentioned in the Will?: Statute contains detailed provisions regarding this matter. Please refer directly to statute text or consult an attorney if this is a critical factor.

Spouse's right to property regardless of Will: Generally, the surviving spouse is entitled to one-half of the deceased spouse's estate if there are no children, and only one-third if there are children. However, please refer directly to the statute as the provisions are detailed.

Community Property or Common Law state?: Common Law.

State restrictions on gifts to charities?: No.

DISTRICT OF COLUMBIA

State Statute or Law description: District of Columbia Code Annotated.

Minimum Age for disposing of property by Will: 18.

Required number of witnesses: Two. (Three are recommended).

May witnesses be beneficiaries?: No.

Are there provisions for Self-Proving Wills?: Yes. (Use the Affidavit form in Chapter 5).

How does Divorce effect the Will?: Generally, revokes the Will.

How does Marriage effect the Will?: Generally, revokes the Will.

Who must be mentioned in the Will?: Surviving spouse.

Spouse's right to property regardless of Will: The surviving spouse is entitled to one-third of the deceased spouse's real estate for the rest of his or her life.

Community Property or Common Law state?: Common Law.

State restrictions on gifts to charities?: No.

GLOSSARY OF LEGAL TERMS

Abatement: a reduction or complete extinguishment of a gift in a Will where the estate does not have sufficient assets to make full payment.

Acknowledgement: formal declaration before a Notary Public.

Ademption: the withdrawal of a gift in a Will by an act of the *Testator's* which shows an intent to revoke it. For example; by giving the willed property away as a gift during his or her life.

Administrator/Administratrix: One who is appointed to administer the estate of a deceased person who has died without a Will or who has died with a Will but has not named an Executor. The distinction between the two titles (male and female) has largely been removed and Administrator is proper usage for either male or female.

Advancement: a lifetime gift made to a child by a parent, with the intent that the gift be all or a portion of what the child will be entitled to on the parent's death.

Ancestor: one from whom a person is descended.

Attestation: to sign one's name as a witness to a Will.

Beneficiary: one who is named in a Will to receive property; one who receives a benefit or gift, as under the terms of a *trust*.

Bequest: traditionally, a gift of personal property in a Will. Synonymous with legacy. Now, "gift" is the appropriate usage for either a gift of real estate or personal property.

Codicil: a formally signed supplement to a Will.

Common Law: system of law which originated in England based on general legal principles rather than legislative acts.

Community Property: the property acquired by either spouse during marriage, other than by gift or inheritance. See Appendix for those states in which this system of marital property applies.

Conservator: temporary court appointed custodian of property.

Curtesy: in ancient common law, a husband's right to all of his wife's real estate for life upon her death. Now generally abolished in most jurisdictions and replaced with a right to a certain *statutory share* of a spouse's property.

Decedent: one who has died.

Descendant: one who is descended from another.

Descent: inheritance by operation of law rather than by Will.

Devise: traditionally, a gift of real estate under a Will. Now, "gift" is the appropriate usage for either a gift of real estate or personal property.

Domicile: a person's principal and permanent home.

Dower: in ancient common law, a wife's right to one-third of her husband's real estate for her life upon his death. Now generally abolished in most jurisdictions and replaced with a right to a certain *statutory share* of a spouse's property.

Escheat: the reversion of property to the state, if there is no family member found to inherit it.

Estate: all property owned by a person.

Execution: the formal signing of a Will.

Executor/Executrix: the person appointed in a Will to carry out the *testator's* wishes and to administer the property.

Fiduciary: a person with a duty of care to another. For example, a *trustee* has a duty of care to any *beneficiary* of a *trust*, and, thus, is a fiduciary.

Gift: a voluntary transfer of property to another without any compensation.

Guardian: a person with the legal power and duty to care for another person and/or a person's property.

Heirs: those persons who inherit from a person by operation of law if there is no Will present.

Holographic: a Will that is entirely handwritten by the *testator*. No longer valid in most states.

Intestate: to die without leaving a valid Will.

Legacy: a gift of personal property in a Will. Now, "gift" is the appropriate usage for either a gift of real estate or personal property. Synonymous with bequest.

Letters of Administration: the court order which officially appoints a person to administer the estate of another.

Letters Testamentary: the court order which officially appoints an *executor* named in a will as the person to administer the estate of the *testator*.

Nuncupative: an oral Will, usually during a person's last illness and later reduced to writing by another. No longer valid in most states.

Per Capita: equally; share and share alike. For example: if a gift is made to ones' descendants, per capita, and one has two children and two grandchildren and one of the children dies, then the gift is divided equally among the surviving child and the two grand-children. This amounts to one-third to the child and one-third to each grand-child.

Per Stirpes: to share by representation. For example: if a gift is made to two children, per stirpes, and one should die but leave two grand-children, the deceased child's share is given to the two grand-children in equal shares. This amounts then to one-half to the surviving child and one-fourth to each of the grand-children.

Personal Property: movable property, as opposed to *real estate*.

Personal Representative: a person who is appointed to administer a deceased's estate. Modern usage which replaces *Executor* and/or *Administrator*.

Posthumous Child: a child born after the father's death.

Pretermitted Child: a child who is left nothing in a parent's will and where there is no intent shown to disinherit.

Probate: the court proceeding to determine the validity of a Will and, in general, the administration of the property which passes under the Will.

Real Estate/Real Property: land and that which is attached permanently to it, as opposed to *personal property*.

Residuary: the remainder of an estate after all debts, taxes, and gifts have been distributed.

Revocation: the annulment of a Will, which renders it invalid. Accomplished either by complete destruction of the original Will or by executing a later Will which revokes the earlier one.

Spouse's Share: (See "*Statutory Share*").

Statutory Share: in "common law" states, that portion of a person's property that a spouse is entitled to by law, regardless of any provisions in a Will.

Testamentary: the expression of intent to dispose of property by Will.

Testator/Testratrix: a male or female who makes a Will.

Trust: in general, property held by one party, the *trustee*, for the benefit of another party, the *beneficiary*.

Trustee: a person appointed to administer a *trust*.

Will: a formally signed and witnessed document by which a person makes a disposition of his or her property to take effect upon death.

INDEX